the
stuff
cure

HOW WE LOST 8,000 POUNDS OF STUFF FOR FUN, PROFIT, VIRTUE, AND A BETTER WORLD

the stuff cure

HOW WE LOST 8,000 POUNDS OF STUFF FOR FUN, PROFIT, VIRTUE, AND A BETTER WORLD

DR. BETTY A. SPROULE AND DR. J. MICHAEL SPROULE

PACIFIC GROVE, CALIFORNIA | NOVEMBER 2012

the stuff cure

HOW WE LOST 8,000 POUNDS OF STUFF FOR FUN, PROFIT, VIRTUE, AND A BETTER WORLD

For more information, visit **www.stuffcure.com**

ISBN-10: 148016237X | ISBN-13: 978-1480162372

PUBLISHED BY MICHELLE MANOS DESIGN | PACIFIC GROVE, CALIFORNIA

Printed in the United States of America

TABLE OF CONTENTS

ACKNOWLEDGEMENTS

Thanks go out to the good folks who've influenced our thinking about stuff. Our parents, Lois and Harold Mathis and Kay and John Sproule, taught the basics of making stuff functional and lasting. Our sons, John and Kevin, helped widen our understanding of stuff across the span of life. From our circle of family and friends across America, we've derived a further wealth of great ideas. Thanks for the help!

We further acknowledge the Professional Organizers who have contributed to our thinking: Krista Clive-Smith, Organized for Life; Isabella Guajardo, Bella Organizing; Cammie Jones, Cammie Jones Organizing; Margaret Lukens, Preparation Nation; Angela Wallace, Wallace Associates; and Joshua Zerkel, Custom Living Solutions. Appreciation, also, to Interior Designers Nancy Bridwell, Bridwell Interior Design; Ken McKelvie, McKelvie Lighting Design; Susan Theodore, Fresh Interiors; Scott Tjaden, Tjaden Interiors; and Tom Williams, Hale-Williams Interior Design. We further recognize Executive Coach, Deb Colden, Deb Colden Executive Consulting and Whole-Life Planners Jim King and Lili Pratt King, Rest of Your Life Institute. Thanks to Michelle Manos, Michelle Manos Design, for producing our book with verve and creativity.

And even after more than 40 years of marriage, we're not taking for granted what is a chance to tip the hat to each other for the fun of completing this book together.

Let's all look forward to a future life with just the right stuff!

Betty and Mike Sproule
Pacific Grove, California

PROLOGUE:
OUR STORY

HOW WE LOST 8,000 POUNDS OF STUFF AND DISCOVERED THE STUFF CURE

If the title of our book tempts you to check out what the Stuff Cure is all about, you're not alone. Millions of Americans share a sense that possessions have heaped up in ways that are hard to manage. But having stuff is fun, too, so the picture can be complicated. Perhaps it will help if we start out by telling you our own story.

Our stuff crisis occurred when we decided to move from a 6,800 square-foot rehabbed Victorian in St. Louis, Missouri to a 1,900 square-foot cottage in Pacific Grove, California. Unlike our prior employer-based moves, this journey of over 2,000 miles would represent an out-of-pocket cost. We realized that expenses would mount as the weight of our stuff was multiplied by the miles transported. And so we wondered: Was it worth the high price to keep all of our current things?

When retaining each pound requires 60¢ or more, the mind becomes concentrated. And so we quickly resolved to slim down the household. As we pared away our store of things, we began to see ourselves embarking upon a "Stuff Cure." We found ourselves using a corresponding verb—"unstuffing"—time and again as we developed ever more specific strategies. Our evolving new vocabulary about stuff became part of rearranging our minds toward a pared-down treatment of possessions. What's more, we discovered that our new array of attitudes and actions could be very satisfying—and even profitable.

This book tells the tale of what we learned on our quest toward a Stuff Cure—how we slimmed down to live an Unstuffed Life. Our California-bound moving van weighed 8,000 pounds less than the truck-full of things that we brought into our St. Louis home a mere four years before. Our story is living proof that the Stuff Cure is something that can work for you.

Reflecting on our experiences, we resolved to share with others what we had learned about living a life unstuffed. You will find us pointing to the fun we had as we planned for leaner living. Here we accomplished the prime objective of saving in moving charges. You may be further interested to learn how we made money by selling or donating excess things. Eventually we pocketed over $10,000 as a combined total of reduced moving costs together with sales of property and income tax savings from charitable donations.

Now, don't get us wrong—most of what we unloaded was far from museum quality. So some of our old things we simply threw out! But the important point to be made about the Stuff Cure is that every form of unstuffing brings its own kind of satisfaction. It is enjoyable simply to see the cleaner shelves and closets when useless clutter goes to recycling or the dumpster. But with our gifts to loved ones, sales to collectors, and donations to charities, the Stuff Cure provided us the further opportunity to make deeper connections with friends, family, and community. Getting ready for our California move represented the beginning of a long-term and meaningful Unstuffed Life. After arriving in our new digs, we continued to refine an ongoing system for assessing possessions and creatively moving along what was unneeded. And we developed new attitudes about how much stuff we really needed to be happy.

The Stuff Cure—whether ours or yours—typically is born of necessity. But the end result is not a one-shot management of crisis—nor is it simply a constant battle against clutter. As we relate the full specifics of the Stuff Cure, you will observe how working for an Unstuffed Life takes you along a path that culminates not only in fun and profit but also in virtue. The part about virtue will become clearer later in the book, but here's a brief explanation for now. The essential virtues of a life cured of clutter spring from our taking less from the planet and giving more to others. It's a formula for doing our part to build a better world by means of steps that, although small in themselves, yet are very real.

We are confident that what we learned will speed your own journey toward the Unstuffed Life. As you pursue personal and family goals following the signposts that we have set up, we further expect to find you believing in the joy of the Stuff Cure.

LOVING AND HATING OUR STUFF

STUFF LOVERS ALL

We're blessed—and it shows in how much we accumulate. The American Way often is taken to mean a lifestyle of more and more. As we continually shop and buy, our orientation to consumership and ownership proves how much we love our stuff!

But then comes the rub. Stuff sometimes seems to take over our lives. Yet because Americans are psychologically more equipped to pile it ON than to move it ALONG, we focus solely on storing the volume of our stuff. Lacking ways to hold down the clutter, the accumulation builds. The longer we live in the same location, the more we pack in. As time passes, we cling to our volumes of stuff as proof of a life filled with rich and varied experiences.

So Stuff—with a capital S—is what this book is about. But we don't see our contribution as merely describing a social problem. We want to share with you our solutions—this is our focus on "Cure." What we call the Stuff Cure can be your guidebook for maximizing what you own. In the chapters to come, we explore the inevitable interplay of pleasures and problems in our life of accumulating and storing things. But ever present is our focus on systematic yet simple ways to manage the accumulation.

It will help to circle back a bit and take a more specific look at our relationship with our stuff. Here we will begin with how we've gotten to where we are, now.

There's Too Much Stuff

It's not hard to find signs of too much stuff in our lives. Just walk around the neighborhood and take a look. Over there we find a neighbor opening the garage door—and what do we see? No car, piles of boxes, with yard and garden paraphernalia propped up in front. A couple houses down, the owners have installed storage shelves—but to no avail. Possessions spill out in front of the shelves. With golf clubs and a disabled bicycle resting against the outside pile, there is still no room for the car. What is important is that the overflowing garages in our neighborhood aren't unique. The National Association of Professional Organizers reports that 25 percent of homeowners with two-car garages don't park any cars in them; 32 percent only have room for one car.[1]

Because our stuff overwhelms garages, closets, shelves, attics, and basements, we rent storage space. The United States now is home to 2.3 billion square feet of self-storage facilities. The Self Storage Association notes that that this total represents more than seven square feet for every man, woman, and child in the nation.[2]

And we're not going to trim down our possessions without some conscious attention. Notwithstanding the Great Recession that began in 2008, Americans developed strong habits of accumulation during the previous forty years when real disposable income per capita doubled. During this time, Americans became accustomed to spending nearly all of it. The result was that, even by the early 1990s, American families were keeping, on average, twice as many possessions as they did 25 years earlier.[3] Accumulation and storage have become part of the culture.

Home — The Place for Our Stuff

George Carlin described the allure of stuff in this way: "That's all we want, that's all you need in life, is a little place for your stuff, ya know?"[4] Carlin's routine became a classic because we recognize it as truth. Personal possessions seem to make us feel whole; they define us and give meaning to our lives.

The notion that stuff accumulates as a kind of giant scrapbook of our lives is reinforced by Thomas Beller's series of essays entitled "The Stuff of Life." Beller focuses on how we view our home and its contents, and he presents "stuff" as an almost derogatory designation for the objects that we have invested with far too much meaning. As a result, the home has become not our personal sanctuary, but rather takes the form of a glorified storage bin for things.[5]

In Beller's telling, stuff does not merely reside in our homes—it is home. Stuff bubbles up when we fill houses and apartments with things not merely functional for living but aspirational in signaling the lives we want to lead. Stuff becomes the tangible element of (a) moments in our past combined with (b) what we want to say about our present. What we buy and keep reflects both pleasant memories and our ability to create an environment of loveliness. Even when things lie about unused, unusable, or inaccessible, we still regard them as evidence of a meaningful past and a hopeful future.

So Carlin is spot on. We don't just have stuff—we love our stuff. We regard stuff as defining who we have become, and how we got there. And, in our mind's eye, even unused things say something potentially important about what we might become—if we could just find or fix what we're not using!

So let's delve a bit more deeply into how we make mere things into the very substance of life.

Shopping and Dropping

A lot of people saw themselves in the 2009 movie "Confessions of a Shopaholic." Self-described shopaholics say that nothing gives them a thrill like flying through the aisles to pluck up new clothes, new shoes, and new jewelry. Dedicated shoppers may admit to having more than they need, already. But this doesn't stop them from ringing up even more whenever something catches their fancy. It's part of the thrill of the hunt—a primitive impulse that calls to us whenever new possessions beckon.

Statistics suggest that we're all shopaholics at heart. And how could it be otherwise? The temptations are ever present—the latest fashions! The new colors for spring! The latest upgrade! The next big thing! Illustrating the power of mere fashion is Boston College sociologist, Juliet B. Schor, who reports that the average American consumer purchased one new piece of clothing every five and a half days.[6] That's 66 purchases per year per person, on average.

Even those of us who feel more restrained still can enjoy a buying spree, especially when on vacation. Tourists are famous not only for eating every kind of ice cream, but for constantly browsing the stands and shops. Even the otherwise sterile environment of the airport offers plenty of retail opportunities that seem to make sense because, whenever we are in transit, we lack access to our full repertoire of stuff.

Without much trouble we find further signs of the ever present impulse to acquire new things. The hundreds of people in the discount stores, the long lines at the checkout, the absence of parking spots—all testify to the universality of the urge to get more. Further reminders that we are not alone in our desire for constant consumption may be seen in the media environment of TV, print, and Internet ads. Pop ups and sidebars on our electronic screens are increasingly personalized to reflect our history of consumption.

And now there's even a musical about shopping, "Shopping! The Musical," written and directed by Morris Bobrow. The show advertises itself with the catchphrase that "the comedy is about everyone's second favorite (and in some cases, favorite) activity."[7]

Our Fashionable Selves

Fashion is a powerful part of what makes it fun to shop as we situate ourselves in an up-to-date cocoon of plenty. It's just not as much fun to wear last year's dress to this year's party! This passion for fashion is long standing and deep seated as shown by Shakespeare's apt observation "The fashion wears out more apparel than the man."[8]

A young woman we know chose a picture for her Facebook profile that pictured her with a very expensive handbag. The picture was really better of the handbag than of her face—so much so that we could identify the brand name of the luxury brand. Here, a fellow stuff lover chose to identify herself by the picture of a handbag, rather than one emphasizing herself.

The universal lure of fashion is not limited to clothes. Fashionable consumption reigns whatever is our particular interest. Some among us love to read about the newest electrical gadgets and impress others by being the first to have the latest-model tech gadget such as iPad, Blackberry, or Nook. Other folks like to drive a car that impresses friends with a luxurious ride.

And we like to have all our stuff at hand in case we need it. So we have a routine for our clothes, our purse, bag, or briefcase. That's part of the reason why we never feel really comfortable in a hotel room—we just don't have all of our stuff nearby.

Bigger Makes for More

The trend toward more and more stuff—and bigger houses to hold it all—is not limited to our own single neighborhood. The average size of newly built homes has steadily increased from just over 1,600 square feet in the late 1970s to nearly 2,300 square feet in 2008—as told by the National Association of Home Builders (NAHB).[9]

It's common for people to dream about having a bigger house—and in no small measure because they need more space for all of their stuff. People proudly display their McMansion with such stuff-oriented features as a three-car garage complete with giant storage cabinets. If they are really lucky, they have a second vacation home as a location for some of the things.

But even those blessed with lots of space find themselves looking for further help against clutter. Just look at stores offering storage solutions. Showrooms brim with brightly colored containers for slicing and dicing our stuff. Complementing magazine advertisement for new bobbles are parallel ads for storage containers and systems. It's not unusual to find an ad for sweaters or shoes on one page with the facing page offering beautiful pictures of a closet system for clothes.

Look around more broadly and you will find self-storage facilities popping up all across the country. In the first decade of the millennium, upward of 3,000 self storage facilities open every year. And no wonder! As shown in a 2006 UCLA study, middle-class families in Los Angeles reported a never ending battle against the overaccumulation, with the most obvious solution being to shift things from overstuffed garages to personal warehouses. The home-storage crisis now extends beyond the home.[10]

And storage has become a general issue in the Western world. First appearing in the United States in the 1960s, storage facilities emerged in London in the 1990s and increasingly are to be found in other parts of Europe. Certainly it will take quite a while for England's 800 self-storage establishments (in 2010) to approximate the 50,000 available in the U.S. However, evidence suggests that external home storage as a general solution to stuff is becoming as permanent in the UK as in the U.S. The Self Storage Association of the United Kingdom reports an ever increasing length of the self-storage contract—from 22 weeks in 2007 to 38 weeks in 2010.[11]

But let's keep in mind the real source of the clutter crisis—it's more fundament than shopping, fashion, and storage. As Pogo, the cartoon figure, once observed: "we have met the enemy, and he is us." Yes, we wouldn't be in this crisis—more stuff, bigger, longer storage—if we didn't love what we are doing.

THE DOWNSIDES OF STUFF

However much we love our things, we all notice when stuff becomes a burden. When layered on, possessions can cause us to act defensively— bringing on bad feelings. Even when we recognize the problem, sometimes we become paralyzed as we struggle to change our behavior and get control over our ever-expanding hoard.

Drawers That Won't Close

Troublesome symptoms of too much stuff crop up everywhere. Our overflowing drawers, jammed closets, and car-free garages reveal the out-of-control stuff life. And if we're one of the lucky ones who have an attic, chances are that we have to turn sideways to walk through the piles.

> ## Top 10 Reasons You Know You Need the Stuff Cure . . .
> ### GOT? . . .
> 10. Unopened boxes from the last move?
> 9. New duplicates of what you can't find?
> 8. Drawers of no return?
> 7. Dining room table never used for meals?
> 6. A TV remote gone AWOL?
> 5. Old purchases still in the wrappers?
> 4. Storage-locker bills due?
> 3. Piles with assigned names?
> 2. A full closet, but nothing to wear?
> 1. A garage never used for the car?

Betty and Mike—your humble authors—used to live in the urban center of a great metropolis where crime—and bad weather—worked hardships on automobiles. Folks in our neighborhood were advised to use "The Club" as a steering-wheel lock to deter casual break-ins. We kept an extra such Club on hand for the autos of overnight guests. Yet one of our neighbors, whose cars were much pricier than ours, always parked on the street. Why was this?

You've probably guessed the answer. Our neighbor couldn't fit either of his two cars in the garage because the space was otherwise occupied by stuff. The stacks and piles in his garage contained the usual—snow blowers, lawn mowers (only some that worked), soccer balls, school projects, and Christmas decorations. We doubted that this mass of material had the value of even a set of new tires for his oldest vehicle.

When soccer balls and Christmas-tree ornaments cause us to put automobiles in harm's way, the mass of our stuff has become a problem. Our neighbor's garage represents what we all recognize as the result of a lifetime of loving to acquire material things—with no particular priority placed on what is really important to keep.

We—and others who have stepped back from the crush of clutter—have begun to recognize that more stuff does not equal more happiness. And that's part of what this book is about. It's time actually to do something about the downsides of clutter. The steps in this book will show how it is possible to have and keep just the right stuff. Yes, it is possible to have everything that is really important to us without feeling burdened by the residue. We'll share what we have learned about reducing the amount of stuff as a step to greater material and spiritual satisfaction.

Stuff as Burden

When we begin to approach stuff defensively, it already has become a burden. Sometimes we don't notice this—others do.

Mavis liked to keep lace doilies over the arms of her chairs in the living room. Reckoning that the arms would show wear first, she reasoned that this precaution would help her maintain a better-looking chair for a longer time. The trouble was that Mavis' daughter, Natalie, thought that the doilies detracted from the overall style of the chairs and—even worse—made the living room look frumpy. Mavis and Natalie argued about the doilies for years. Memories of the arguments lasted longer than either the chairs or the doilies.

Our thoughts also turn to Hannah, who believed in the concept of "too nice to use." This meant that something was so special that it should only be used for extraordinary occasions. Hannah's children would outgrow clothes that were practically brand new because they were "too nice to wear." Hanna's savoring of pristine clothing made fashion unavailable for actual wearing, with the results that her children felt especially guilty if something nice was torn or got dirty.

So a clear sign that stuff is become a burden is when we feel an ongoing need to protect things by hiding them away unused. Maybe it would be better to start reconsidering our basic attitude towards what we possess.

Stuff Complicates Relationships

Attitudes towards stuff figure prominently in relationships. Mavis's and Natalie's lifelong argument about arm-chair doilies, mentioned above, shows the danger of privileging things over people. When treated as treasure, very ordinary stuff may become the focus of relationship conflicts.

The classic 1989 movie, "When Harry Met Sally," presents us with a memorable scene where the recently divorced Harry (played by Billy Crystal) advises his friends, Jess and Marie, as they work to merge their stuff into one household. The would-be newlyweds are arguing about a wagon-wheel coffee table that Jess loves but that Marie simply won't have in her home.

Harry finally blurts out: "Everything's fine, everybody's in love, everybody's happy—and before you know it, you're screaming at each other about who owns the stereo. Some day you'll be fighting over this dish. I mean it. I mean it. Put your name in your books. Now, while you're unpacking them, before they get all mixed up together and you can't remember whose is whose. Because someday, believe it or not, you're going to be fighting over who's going to get this coffee table, this stupid wagon wheel coffee table."[12]

It's a great scene because it rings true. And it's not just in movies where stuff can be the source of relationship hassles. One young couple we know argued at length about whether he should buy a special car to drive in auto-cross races. The car cost money, took up space—and, moreover, monopolized a lot of the husbands' time. The wife, who yearned for a baby, didn't want her husband away at the auto-cross events for days on end. Both had their point of view—and the extra car became the sore spot of the argument.

Another proverbial occasion where stuff becomes an issue is cleaning up the house for company. This is where all of the "his stuff" and "her stuff" issues come to the fore. And after the party, comes the related question of who put what where.

Our attitudes about stuff are formed in early childhood—from the time we learn to say "it's mine." Corresponding is a lifetime of hearing others say "be careful with it." Yes, relationships are influenced by how we manage stuff. And it's not always pretty.

COPING WITH THE TYRANNY OF STUFF

As shown by the proliferation of storage units, acquired stuff tends to stick. Even when we summon up the courage to move a few things along, we're always held back by the problem of where to start.

Often, the first sign that we're ready to think seriously about cutting down the clutter is a recurring general uneasiness about mounting piles. Here we are beginning to feel the tyranny of possessions as it all builds up in layers. What we are sensing is that material objects, once intended to support our life, now actually are in control. Our consumption now consumes us. What formerly empowered us now presents us with a burden.

And so we cast about for a way to lighten the mental load brought on by Too Much Stuff. Individually, and in families, we all have a strategy for dealing with the monster of too-muchness. So we store things; or we try a spring cleaning. The trouble with these two approaches is that they are usually painfully ad hoc and often merely rearrange or postpone the problem.

Not by Storage Alone

Stuff expands to fill the available storage space. This is a principle that could be added to Newton's list of physical laws. We offer our own Stuff Life as a case in point.

Long before we made the move to California, we got the first hints that there might be a problem in our family Stuff Life. As newlyweds, we set up early housekeeping in the American Midwest. Midwestern homes frequently facilitate simple storage as a solution to the problem of accumulation. We enjoyed the luxury of being able to put excess things in the attic, the basement, and the garage. No anxiety or arguments. Out of sight and out of mind. Problem solved.

Or was it? We eventually learned that storage only postponed the problem. As time passed, the storage spaces above and below became so packed—and the garage so full—that a stuff crisis emerged. This first harbinger of a problem supplied the motivation for some of our earliest thinking about how to rid ourselves of things unnecessary.

Not Just by Spring Cleaning

So, like many, we tried spring cleaning. But we discovered that cleaning-up invariably brought nagging-about. We disagreed not only about what was "junk" but also what was meant by "clean." Worse yet, our few painfully achieved gains didn't last very long. Bottom Line: It was just too hard to find a win by sprucing things up. It was less painful to do nothing—as in the story of the woman who combed her long hair but once a year. She found it so painful; she couldn't imagine how anyone could do it everyday.

Everyone, of course, has his or her own particular gimmick for coping with a stuff crisis. Our friend, Samantha, brightly bragged to us one day that she had a surefire way to motivate spring cleaning—at least as regarded her garage. She used the incentive of buying a new car—and the associated desire to keep the new car in the garage—as her leverage point. The family would car-shop for weeks to see the new models with the latest exciting features. When they found a car they all liked, Samantha would announce, "We can't get a new car till we clean out the garage." Then came a family work day to sort through stuff, throw a few things out, and finally hose down the interior.

The trouble with Samantha's solution is that her family didn't buy cars very often. Their garage was often filled with junk within a few weeks of bringing home the new car. Garage storage was a problem never really solved. Not to mention the fact that Samantha's temporarily clean garage did nothing for her overstuffed basement or attic!

THERE IS A CURE

So it seems pretty clear that the experience of Too Much Stuff is well nigh universal—and it's not something easily solved. Stuff is like air—something always around—and we take the whole process for granted as we want things, shop for them, bring them home, use them for a while, store them, and then occasionally even try to get rid of them.

It will be hard to approach the stuff crisis with measures that rise above the halfhearted or occasional as long as we regard possession as normal and de-acquisitioning as exceptional. So that's where the Stuff Cure comes in. The story of this book is about a higher level of managing our things—and having fun in the process.

We use the term, "Stuff Cure" as shorthand for success in handling the accumulation of things. The book relates our discoveries that began when we realized that Too Much Stuff represented a real crisis. We'll show you how we gradually became better able to formulate clear objectives for moving along excess things—and how we took note of our key learnings at each stage. We'll share how we found the joy in getting rid of stuff, and how we experienced additional pleasure in living without the burden of excess.

Our bottom line for you is this: The book that you hold in your hands is a proven way to turn cleaning and organizing chores into a permanent cure for clutter. You'll master an approach that has given us hours of fun and has opened up opportunities for profit, virtue, and making a better world. Our book represents our invitation for you to join in this journey.

2

WHY STUFF CLINGS

When Betty finished work on her master's degree, she had a copy of her thesis bound as a gift for her professor, Dr. Jack. Because he was leaving the university shortly after spring graduation, Betty made an appointment to give him the gift. When she went to Dr. Jack's office to present the bound copy, he was pleased to receive it, and Betty enjoyed Dr. Jack's kind words about her work as a graduate student. Dr. Jack emphasized that he wanted to put her thesis in a special place so that it wouldn't get lost in his move.

What was this special place? Dr. Jack pivoted his chair to an open box, placed Betty's thesis inside, and taped it up. He took up a black marking pen and carefully hand-lettered the label: "STUFF."

Even recalling the incident, Betty still feels a little hurt that her laboriously prepared thesis was relegated to a box with the nonexclusive and uninformative label of "Stuff." Dr. Jack must have seen the look of disappointment on Betty's face; and he reassured her, not too persuasively, that "things we label 'Stuff' are very precious to me." And he added: "It's not a term I use lightly." At least Dr. Jack hadn't labeled the box "Junk."

Clearly, Dr. Jack didn't regard Betty's thesis as precious enough to deserve a special label, or even a very specific one. For Dr. Jack, Betty's work apparently fell into a general tale of his years spent at the university. But for Betty, this specially prepared copy of her master's study was the centerpiece of a very particular and special story of her life as a student. The work was so close to Betty's heart that she even saved the heavy IBM punch cards on which it, originally, had been prepared.

EVERYTHING HAS A STORY

We don't know whether Dr. Jack still is in possession of Betty's bound thesis, but she kept those old punch cards for years—even after they had become so obsolete as to be unreadable by any computer outside of the Smithsonian Institution. But for the accident of a basement flood, we would probably still be hanging onto them yet today!

Retaining paper computer cards in the Internet age represents perhaps the ultimate case of useless, obsolete stuff clinging to our forward-moving lives.

What is the underlying principle here? What is the fundamental attraction that causes stuff to cling? Why do we feel pangs of regret when we think of getting rid of something forever? Why do we surround ourselves with once-functional items that have long lost their usefulness?

Let's take a stab at these questions. Because we all attribute meaning to obsolete objects, it appears that stuff clings chiefly because it reminds us of the story of our lives. Material objects conjure up feelings and memories that, together, constitute our humanity. When looked at, or thought about, the items that we keep enable us to clarify what our experiences of living add up to.

Let's test this idea that stuff symbolically represents life. Pick an object that you're really embarrassed to still have—maybe something that you've considered getting rid of, or a thing that somebody else has advised you to throw away. It's highly likely that you'll find this object serving as an entry point to important life memories.

As you think about this questionable item in your household inventory, try asking yourself these questions:

Q. Where were you when you got it? Was it a gift or something you bought?

Q. If you bought it, how much did it cost? Did you have plans for using the item?

Q. How did the object make you feel when you got it? Are these feelings connected to relationships that you have with other people?

If you're like most people, one or more these questions caused memories of your life to flash before you.

To further clarify what is going on, your authors will apply the above questions to something in our own stuff life—two well-worn, matching Samsonite suitcases that we had kept in our closet for over 35 years.

Q. Where were you when you got it? Was it a gift or something you bought?
A. Mike's parents gave him the matched luggage as a high-school graduation gift.

Q. If you bought it, how much did it cost? Did you have plans for using the item?
A. At the time, this set was the latest in luggage and Mike used it to pack his things for college and then later for his first trip to Europe.

Q. How did the object make you feel when you got it? Are these feelings connected to relationships that you have with other people?
A. Although Mike didn't attend the kind of high school where graduates expected a new car, a commencement gift of luggage still represented his parent's practical and thrifty approach to life. He recognized, also, that the gift signaled their loving confidence that Mike was ready for a world of new adventures.

For years after Mike's old suitcases became barely useable, they still served to remind us of the trips Mike took from home to college, his first and second trip to Europe, and even our honeymoon.

It seems to be the case that personal stories—complete with details and emotions—become attached to even neglected or nonfunctional parts of our stuff inventory. So that's the problem in a nutshell: lose the stuff, lose the memory. Or at least that's what we fear. So we hold onto the core of our being when we keep on hand physical objects that have traveled with us on our journey.

This exercise shows that the Stuff Cure represents an emotional as well as physical journey. Feelings come forth when we begin to make decisions about what to keep and what to pitch. So we need to remember the fundamental sentimentality of stuff when we first think about reducing our stock. Yes, we feel attachments to stuff—but this is normal.

Moreover, sentiment need not paralyze action. It's possible to cure clutter even as we love stuff. But it's going to require changing some habits.

HABITS OF HOLDING ON

People typically settle into habits of holding on to stuff long past the point of actual usefulness. Do you recognize some of the following telltale behavioral or attitudinal signs? Specifically, do you find yourself (1) squirreling things away? (2)

always seeking out more? (3) guilt-tripping yourself for disposing of gifts received? (4) keeping unwanted stuff as a memorial to loved ones? (5) treating unused stuff as central to a deferred dream? and/or (6) letting clutter overwhelm?

All six of these holding-on habits are common—and many may date from early childhood. Changing ingrained behaviors and attitudes is going to require some serious commitment!

Below, we will review with you each of the six Habits of Holding On introduced above. In each case, check to see whether—and to what extent—a given habit causes you to cling to otherwise undesirable things.

Squirreling Things Away

An eight-year-old was asked to give advice to another child who would soon become a big brother. Knowing what it was like to find a favorite toy broken or missing, the eight-year-old answered, "Hide your stuff."

Everyone can remember when a sibling or friend mishandled and ruined one of our favorite things. So it's a constant struggle for parents who want to teach their children how to play nicely and share toys. The habit of keeping things squirreled away from others is a lesson learned early in life. From childhood, we began to think that storing things is the best way to keep them intact and ready to use.

Always Wanting More

Not only do we learn to store away what we have, but life seems to teach us the related lesson that, when it comes to stuff, more is better. Our friend, Mason, enjoys wine and everything connected to wine. He travels to wineries and, after participating in a tasting, buys whole cases. Then Mason needs to have just the right glasses to serve each variety of wine. Up next is maintaining and upgrading the wine cellar. Mason now has a stock of over 3,000 bottles.

Even with no further wines purchased, it's going to take Mason a lifetime or more to consume his collection. But Mason is not deterred by the knowledge that he'll never drink some of this favorite wine. Part of the fun of Mason's life is his anticipating that next great bottle.

Mason's ever expanding wine collection illustrates how we keep adding to an already excessive stuff inventory. The craving for more things is like the urge to consume delicious food even when we're no longer hungry. Furthermore, just as an overstuffed stomach requires some relief, our overstocked drawers, closets, and garages call for a cure.

Guilt from Disposing of Gifts Received

Sometimes we keep things in the spirit of loyalty. We are particularly likely to apply a loyalty test to gifts received from family and friends. Arguably, getting rid of a present represents our betraying someone we love or respect. In this way, a pin that Betty received from her aunt at high school graduation marked a shared sense of family accomplishment. Thirty years later, the value of the pin lies more in the memory than in the metal.

We use "the cut flowers test" as a way of dealing with the guilt that crops up when we contemplate disposing of old gifts lying around unused and/or unwanted. Our thoughts turn to people who have given us fresh flowers. After a few days, when the flowers have faded, we find ourselves quite able to throw away the wilted blossoms without compunction. In this case, both receiver and benefactor clearly expected that the bouquet would only be pretty for a few days. Thus, neither party would sense that something was amiss when the flowers retire to the composting bin.

When you think about it, the "cut flowers" test can be applied to any gift. The trick is to remember that the giver originally wanted to make our life more beautiful. Perhaps a better way to honor this sentiment would be to move the gift along to someone who might better use it or appreciate it.

Keeping Stuff as a Memorial

Objects inherited from the estate of a loved one may carry particular emotion; therefore, disposing of such an item may weigh more heavily on our conscience.

Ann's mother, Veronica, very often made cornbread to go with dinner. Daughter Ann treasures her inherited cornbread pan because of it was a daily part of her mother's household routine; and it conjures up memories of Ann's life when she was a little girl. Even though Ann doesn't make cornbread as often as her mother did, there's no way she will ever part with that cast iron pan.

But what happens when we are the beneficiaries of boxes upon boxes of items reputed to have belonged to this or that departed relative or close friend? A few of these items are—like Ann's cornbread pan—something that no one would ever, ever part with. But sometimes the sheer volume of estate material almost demands that we look for ways, respectfully, to move along some of the stuff.

Using a family-oriented version of the "cut flowers" test, we have gradually pared down our own inherited bric-a-brac. We have tried to reposition some of the pieces to others in the family who would value them even more. For instance, some of Mike's mother's china, silver, and jewelry were gladly received by cousins and nieces. Other items have made fine donations to charity gift shops and auctions that exist to support causes that our ancestors would be proud of.

But don't get us wrong. As with Ann's cornbread pan, we ourselves are keeping a firm hold of certain heirlooms. One example is a small dish made of porcelain that is hand painted. We don't particularly like the style of the dish or the design, but we have kept it throughout our life because family lore has it that this piece once belonged to Betty's great-grandmother. Except for a picture, we have no other tangible experience of Betty's grandmother's mother other than the dish. And because Betty's family had few fancy things, we assume that this otherwise undistinguished porcelain piece must have been greatly treasured by Betty's forebearers.

So, yes, stuff clings even for practitioners of the Stuff Cure. But even though we all have items that we are keeping strictly for the sentimentality, there are a couple of important things to remember from a Stuff-Cure point of view. First, winnow down estate items to those most important. Second, try not to lay a guilt trip on succeeding generations who may not share your own sentimentality about an item. Here's a tip: If you want your kids to treasure an item to the extent you do, then bring it out and use it so that they will have personal memories associated with it.

Treating Stuff As Deferred Dream

Clinging to stuff not only responds to feelings about the past, but our store of things also reflects aspirations for the future.

It's not hard to find examples of stuff maintained for a dreamed-of future life. Unsophisticated photographers have been known to stash expensive camera equipment in the closet for that day when they'll—finally—become photographic experts. Then there are those who are holding on to dinner service for 24 on account of the Great-Gatsby-type banquets they plan to host—someday. Sports enthusiasts have been known to accumulate equipment—such as for scuba diving—for that dreamed-of first trip to Mexico or Club Med.

Sometimes clinging to things represents a merger of past memories and future hopes. It's not uncommon to retain clothes that we wore before we gained weight against the possibility that, someday, when we lose weight, they'll fit us again. Meanwhile the clothes hang in our closet as fodder for moths or for a retro-dressing party.

Letting Clutter Overwhelm

Sometimes clinging to things simply represents serially safeguarding what seems important in the constant flow of material coming at us. Everyday our mailboxes fill with third- and fourth-class fliers, papers, and envelopes that beckon us to "open immediately!" Sometimes advertising fliers are crassly disguised by labels that identify them as "registered mail" or "important financial documents." It doesn't take long to accumulate quite a pile even when we just keep what is marked "urgent!"

Our local news media reported a sad story about a resident whose kitchen suffered an electrical fire. The house was so cluttered with books, paper, boxes and debris that the firefighters could not gain access—and the excess paper contributed to the blaze. First responders testified that the flames could have been contained with limited damage had it not been for the overabundance of clutter.[1]

WHEN STUFF CLINGS—AND WHEN IT DOESN'T

CLINGS:
When old stuff represents, even replaces life.

DOESN'T CLING:
Keeping just the right stuff to make space for new stories.

COPING BUT NOT CURING

Because stuff clings to us with all its might, no wonder people are seeking a
way to manage the super-abundance of things. Most people we know sense that
they are holding onto too many possessions in their lives. However, the norm in
our circle is to avoid talking about clutter. People recognize that it is somewhat
unseemly to complain that the blessing of stuff brings, also, a burden.

Even if we don't talk about it, the desire to manage the multitude of things seems
to be universal in affluent societies. Yet successful stuff management can be a rarity
given the many reasons that our stuff clings. The seeds of this present book were
planted when we began to visit a wider range of homes in the context of parent
gatherings for children's activities and events. More and more it dawned on us
that clutter was not a problem for the few but rather was a challenge for everyone.
We were motivated to think more systematically about solutions that go beyond
hoping and coping. These observations became the kernel of what we call The
Stuff Cure.

But let us return, briefly, to the idea that sweeping a problem under the rug is not
the same as really cleaning it up. Coping is not curing.

In our own quest for the Stuff Cure, we noticed that we and others typically turn
to a characteristic set of unsuccessful approaches to reduce the piles of stuff. Below
we headline these approaches as:
> (1) letting someone else deal with it;
> (2) procrastinating;
> (3) burying treasures;
> (4) fussing and arguing; and
> (5) wishful resolving.

Letting Someone Else Deal with It
Mike's Great, Great Aunt Clyda developed a strategy for coping with her stuff that
worked for her—but that wasn't so good for her relatives. She kept everything
she ever owned—which was a lot in view of her artistic interests and hobbies.
Squirreling away was fine for Aunt Clyda; however, when she died in the 1960s,
her heirs were faced with a house packed full of costume jewelry boxes, plated
silverware turned black from disuse—even a disabled Model T Ford in the garage.
This enormous job included disposing of racks full of theatrical costumes dating

back to the 1890s.

In the same spirit of deferring the clutter cleanup, our friend, Aidan, enjoys visualizing his kids coping with his stuff-filled house. The piles would represent parental revenge for what his children put him through as teenagers. Comments about this dream draw far more laughter from Aidan than from the offspring.

Faced with a mountain of material, one family called in professionals to clean up the house of a deceased relative. The experts worked full-time for three weeks to sort through all the stuff, looking both for valuable possessions and the papers need to settle the estate. The final bill for the clean-up was over $20,000. Sadly, the consultants were no more successful than the relatives in finding anything of value.[2]

For the sake of the family, it may be well to think of what our heirs will face when disposing of our material estate. Rather than leaving unsorted piles and packed closets, why not simultaneously conquer clutter and increase joy by transforming excess things into welcomed gifts? In any event, simply keeping up-to-date with our material bounty will be a true gift to our loved ones.

Procrastinating

Some of us hold in mind's eye the image of super, duper spring cleaning just ahead. This vision lessens our sense of a need to deal with everything lying around. It seems perfectly clear that, someday in the future, we will organize the ultimate work day that will finally purge the excess stuff. But when we take a realistic look at such a dream, many of us will admit not only that the vision may be unrealistic, but that this dream carries with it the dread that we are merely postponing Herculean labors. It's easier to keep our heads down, on a day-to-day basis, and just live with too much stuff.

Here's a test: How much work would it be to get your house organized enough to invite over some folks that you'd like to impress? The National Association of Professional Organizers *www.napo.net* did a survey on their website asking respondents "How long would take you to get your house ready for dinner guests?" Two thirds of respondents replied that they would be ready in four hours or less. Over 20 percent of respondents answered that it would take between eight and 40 hours. More than ten percent answered that they would never invite anyone inside their house! The moral of the story is that nearly everybody feels behind in organizing their things.

Burying Treasures

In addition to sloughing off and procrastinating, another coping strategy is to put stuff out of sight and mind—bury it—in drawers, piles, boxes, closets, and storerooms.

Our friend, Lauren, has a drawer she calls the "drawer of no return" where she puts things that are not terribly useful but that she wants to hold onto—just in case. Trouble is, Lauren has a growing collection of such drawers.

Putting stuff in piles is another version of burying the treasures. Having the stuff neatly stacked makes some of it disappear, at least for the time being. And scooping the pile into a box or storage container to be sorted later seems to be the logical follow-up expedient. But, as with drawers, the multiplication principle applies to boxes and storage units.

David thought he had a solution far better than drawers, piles, and containers. He put a dumpster-size personal storage unit on his driveway. But it wasn't long before he learned of the city ordinance permitting storage units to remain in driveways for a maximum of three days before citations were to be issued.

Sally thought she had a solution in the form of several off-site storage lockers. Well, there was the slight problem of cost. But to hide the expense from her husband, Sally paid the storage locker bills from her personal checking account. And Sally is not alone in renting an off-site garage-type storage unit. There are an estimated 51,000 storage facilities in the U.S.—more than seven times the number of Starbucks coffee shops.[3]

Of course we should not forget the inconvenience of having our possessions stored off site in what is probably a haphazard pile of boxes. But as with Sally's situation of hiding costs from her husband, the real stumbling block of commercial storage is the mounting expense. As a result, many people are now walking away from their units—such a great number, that television shows now are built around abandoned storage lockers.

Reality-show bidding wars notwithstanding, the entire contents of lockers are usually sold for between \$10 and \$200 to persons hoping to cash in on one or two valuable items. The rest, of course, is simply thrown out by the new owners. Truly this is a cruel fate for family photos and other treasures that, just a few months ago, we couldn't bear to part with.[4]

Fussing and Arguing

In his classic comedy routine on stuff, George Carlin gives us this great insight. "Have you noticed that THEIR stuff is shit and YOUR shit is stuff? God! And you say, 'Get that shit offa there and let me put my stuff down!'"[5]

The case of Jenny and Mike Arbanas illustrates the treasure vs. trash dilemma that surrounds the stuff held onto by different persons in a relationship. It seems that Mike's collection of hunting trophies crops up frequently in this couple's conversations—particularly his stuffed wild turkeys. Mike loves to hunt, and on a trip to South Dakota, he bagged two wild turkeys. He was so proud of his accomplishment that he took his game trophies to a taxidermist who mounted them at a cost of over \$900. His wife, Jenny, thought the birds mounted on pedestals amounted to a monstrosity, and she didn't want them in their home. In a compromise, the turkeys were relegated to a den used chiefly by Mike. But the mounted game trophies continue to be a sore spot for the couple.[6]

We know a couple, the Bensons, who have taken fussing and arguing to the next level. Instead of verbal barbs, they use the scoop-and-carry approach. Theirs is a truly hands-on method for dealing with too much stuff. One of the pair, usually wife Jenny, takes an offending item out to the garage—things she views as too-long unused or entirely useless. If the other partner, usually husband Craig, hasn't returned an item from the garage within a month, then the material is subject to being donated. Mrs. Benson seems far more satisfied with this approach than Mr. Benson.

Wishful Resolving

The dream of a magical clean-up day tends to surface at the beginning of every year. No wonder that January has been named our nation's official get-organized month. In published surveys, "Getting Organized" has made the list of Top 10 resolutions for many years. We predict it will still be on the list in 2020. On

January 10, 2011 an article appeared in the *New York Times* entitled "Organize This."[7] The title and contents proved so intriguing that, by the next day, this article with its tips for clearing out clutter had been emailed so frequently that it made the top-three list for articles forwarded for that date.

We can recognize this wishful approach to clutter because we have lived it. In the early years of our marriage, despite periodic clean-ups, clutter seemed to grow in certain corners of our house like "The Blob." Particularly notorious was one particular desk in the basement game room that was home to papers stacked three feet high in rows of piles. Facing this desk was a Harry Potter-type space under the staircase that gradually became designated as "The Boxes Closet." Behind a neighboring door, we invested in shelving for our large utilities room, but soon these cheap steel units began to sag.

The real problem for us was not space or furniture, but rather too much stuff. And it's an almost universal condition among persons living in developed market economies. The phenomenon of Too Much Stuff has become a social truism whether we consider our own Boxes Closet, or David's driveway storage module, or Sally's serial off-site units. It's simply hard to be organized without reducing the old inventory and mounting a campaign to manage the new inflow. And this is what the Stuff Cure is all about.

TOWARD A REAL CURE

Looking at how people live their stuff lives, it becomes clear that we need a better approach to clutter than the old standbys. Expedients just don't seem to work, whether we try sloughing off or procrastinating, whether we bury things in boxes and units, or fuss with each other, or whether we periodically or annually resolve to clean things up.

COPING BUT NOT CURING
Letting Someone Else Deal with It
Procrastinating
Burying Treasures
Fussing and Arguing
Wishful Resolving

What we are sharing with you—The Stuff Cure—represents an array of attitudes with associated behaviors. But everything is closely focused on the Big Picture, that is, how to acquire, use, and enjoy things without becoming burdened with bounty.

Right now, it is sufficient to say that the Cure relies on two fundamental changes to our behavior—two actions linked to an overall attitude. The action agenda involves (1) depleting inventories and (2) displacing things. The corresponding attitude is one of wanting to have just the right stuff.

Depleting Inventories

When Mike moved his mother out of the family home, he found himself disposing of things whose usability had expired or that had been saved up in such great abundance as to preclude normal depletion. Representing the category of "things expired" were soft drinks so old that there was no fizz when the cans were opened. The only solution was to pour out the limp liquid and recycle the aluminum.

Illustrative of excess inventory were the many unopened Kleenex boxes stuffed into cabinets and closets all over the house. So many tissue boxes emerged during the packing process that Mike was unable to fit all of them into the car at the time of the last load-up. He had to hide some of these boxes in the garage so that his frugal mom wouldn't see that they were being abandoned.

What this story proves is that too much stockpiling can be wasteful, and therefore costly. Consumables such as soft drinks age and depreciate, and so should be kept handy for ongoing usage. But even shelf-stable goods—such as paper products— lose value when we lose track of how much inventory we have.

Mike's experience alerted us to the potential that having a smaller storehouse of consumable stuff actually could save us money. This was a first step toward seeing the real value of empty space on shelves and in closets. This realization further motivated us to expand the idea of a smaller inventory. It seemed to us that the principle of "keeping less on hand" could be applied to nearly everything we owned.

And once we got started thinking seriously about the accumulation of stuff, we looked for—and found—two further principles closely associated with a smaller household stockpile.

The Displacement Idea

A corollary to after-the-fact inventory-reduction is ongoing displacement. Displacement represents the principle of "one-in, one-out"; in other words, getting rid of something once you buy its duplicate. So that when you bring home the new bicycle, you don't automatically put the old one in the basement or the storage shed. Perhaps it might be donated or otherwise moved along usefully. In this way, shopping doesn't inevitably bring about the proliferation of stuff.

The poster-adult for the idea of displacement is our friend, Carter, who lives in a 150-square foot apartment. The ever-visible four walls of his place keep him focused on a careful recipe detailing what he really needs. Carter finds that "in-with-the-new/out-with-the-old" enables him to live comfortably in his small space.

Just the Right Stuff

Common to depleting inventory and displacing duplicates is an attitude that values "the right stuff" over "more stuff." As we practiced depleting and displacing, we reassessed what was located where. Our goal was to situate necessary stuff in "prime real estate," that is, places close at hand.

The focus on prime possessions in key places first came into play in the kitchen. We checked to make sure that frequently used pots and pans were easily accessible in the cabinet under the cook top. We didn't have to make too many changes, here; but our kitchen proved to be less well organized in relation to duplicates and infrequently used items. So we purged drawers of unnecessary multiples, for example, getting rid of a half-dozen dull potato peelers.

We likewise freed up space in "prime real estate" by locating our rarely used cherry pit remover, and other such items, more remotely.

Now we were getting excited about the prospect of really "unstuffing" our lives. We would keep what was most important—and get rid of the rest. We would apply to the whole house the principles we first used for the kitchen, that is, no duplicates, no broken and nonfunctioning utensils, and the most used things in the handiest places.

The three basics of depletion, displacement, and right stuff/right place convey only the outlines of what we have termed the Stuff Cure; but their importance cannot be overstated. They represent what is missing in those ads for bins, containers, and closet storage systems. Now there's no question that a closet system adds value—we've installed them in our own kids' rooms. But contrary to the pictures of a system-organized wardrobe, most people will be stuffing into the closet a lot more than the five blouses, two coats, and four skirts depicted in the advertisement. So even with a closet system, it's going to be necessary to reduce excess inventory and displace on an ongoing basis whatever is outmoded.

Yes, there are so many reasons that stuff clings—and we've tried to help you tally them up. It's almost contrary to human nature for us to let things go. We dream of future uses. We experience the emotional connection to items that symbolize our lives and loved ones. But the situation is far from hopeless as shown by the three related principles of depleting, displacing, and organizing our rooms around just the right stuff.

BEHAVIORS FOR A REAL CURE
Deplete Inventories
Displacement: IN with the New, OUT with the Old
An Attitude of Just the Right Stuff

In the chapters that follow, we'll show you how to travel beyond these three guideposts as you journey toward your own Stuff Cure. We'll begin by sharing key criteria for what to keep and what to move along. We'll show you the many viable and desirable alternatives to letting stuff pile up. We'll lay out easy-to-use steps for organizing the right stuff in its proper place—room by room. And we'll demonstrate how the slimmed-down approach to possessions builds healthy human relationships and helps bring about the brighter future we seek for ourselves and others.

3

KNOWING WHAT TO KEEP

When carving the statue of David, Michelangelo felt that he could actually see David's form standing in the marble. So the task became that of simply removing all the extra stone surrounding the statue. The Stuff Cure operates on the same principle. We prune away what's not needed by visualizing what's essential. The Stuff Cure is all about having just the right stuff by getting rid of the excess.

In this spirit, on the twentieth anniversary of our marriage, we thought it was finally time to take a thorough review our wedding gifts. We wondered if we were keeping anything clearly expendable. For years, we had set aside a special space—that we called our "Boxes Closet"—just for storing wedding presents. Most were still in their original gift packages. Now was the opportunity to take an updated look at what our friends and family thought we needed long ago. Our plan was to open each box and decide whether each item was a "keeper" or was dispensable.

WHAT IS A "KEEPER?"

What proved to be our first stumbling block was our lack of any explicit rules of thumb for what we would hold onto. It quickly became apparent that we needed criteria to apply to the large stack of boxed mementos from our special day. Gradually, as we gained more experience going through the boxes, specific guidelines began to emerge that sped our progress in deciding what was essential. Eventually, we resolved that if a gift failed to pass muster with respect to at least one of the emerging criteria, then we would put it in our next garage sale or donation.

Yet it took a while for us to develop a process for deciding what to keep and what to dispose of. So, it may be helpful at this point for us to circle back and explain how we derived three key criteria for separating the essentials from the expendables.

Shrimp Forks, Anyone?

One of our first re-discoveries in the Boxes Closet was a set of six gold-plated shrimp forks. You might think that it would be easy to decide whether to keep or dispense with this never-used gift from a friend who now lived 2000 miles away. But we soon found ourselves chatting on about the beauty of the forks, their unique function on a dinner table, et cetera. After 25 minutes of discussion—with no decision yet—we realized that unstuffing our Boxes Closet would not be easy.

In retrospect, what we thought was a simple discussion about shrimp forks instead represented an entry point to a larger journey of discovery having both personal and relationship dimensions. This bigger picture became clearer as we regrouped to ask ourselves a series of tougher questions. For starts: "Would we ever use the shrimp forks?" If we hadn't used them in two decades, maybe that meant they weren't really functional for us with our current lifestyle. The shrimp forks were beginning to become candidates for unstuffing.

Yet after a bit more discussion, we began to waiver. We reprised the idea that maybe we might be serving shrimp at some point in the future. Then the conversation shifted back to the fact that we had owned the shrimp forks for a fifth of a century without ever having set them on the table. Glancing at the clock, we noted the irony that our obsessing about the forks already had occupied more time than would be required to eat a barrel-full of shrimp—with or without forks. The more we talked, seemingly the harder the decision became.

So we tried another tack. "Were the forks valuable?" Maybe they weren't gold plated, but solid gold. Maybe collectors in the future would want them as an example of lifestyle in the 1970s. Maybe at some point in the future we would sell them at a garage sale for several times what they had cost. But all these "maybes" seemed to reflect merely wishful thinking—the vain hope that we owned something having significant worth.

Forging ahead, we turned to another line of thinking focused more on sentiment. We remembered our friend, Helen, who presented the shrimp forks to us at the time of our wedding. What if Helen came to visit and asked us about her gift? Would sentiments toward our friend or memories of our wedding cause us to regret disposing of the forks?

As we asked these and other questions about the shrimp forks, we began to fear that we wouldn't be able to significantly cleanse the Boxes Closet. Were we going to be stymied by six small utensils?

The Three Criteria

But all of our questioning pointed us, at least, along a path of progress. As we accumulated some serious discussion time, we realized that we were settling upon three primary criteria to help us make our decisions. These three criteria had to do with questions of (1) functionality, (2) value, and (3) sentimentality.

Is it functional? All our comments about "maybe this" and "maybe that" brought home the point that real usefulness relates to the present. We began to ask whether what we owned was something currently used in our everyday lives. Things failing the test included clothes that didn't fit, broken combs, and aspirin with a decade-old expiration date.

Is it valuable? To get our heads wrapped around the idea of value, we asked this question: Could an object be sold for at least $100? Better yet, would someone be willing to pay us $500? Here it is important to keep focus on the principle that value, like beauty, is in the eye of the beholder. In this spirit, Mike's father operated his antiques business on the basis that an object's true value was what a real person was willing to pay for it right now. He recognized that actual purchasers wouldn't care about what he originally had paid for something or what it sold for elsewhere or at another time. The same holds true for everything we own. In estimating value, we shouldn't project unrealistic assumptions about any "proper" or ideal worth. Value is based on the purchaser's perspective, right now.

Is it sentimental? Things sentimental are precious to us because of what they represent in our lives. Here our emotional connection to objects does not necessarily depend on their utility or sale value. Almost everything we own has a story and, therefore, carries a degree of sentiment. So application of the criterion of sentiment finds us questioning whether something is especially meaningful.

These then were the three criteria that we derived for WHAT TO RETAIN:

Currently functional?
Really valuable?
Outrageously sentimental?

As we sorted through our things, we found it useful to keep repeating these three questions as a kind of mantra for the Stuff Cure.

But criteria are theoretical. The real test of the Stuff Cure is actually applying questions of functionality, value, and sentiment to specific objects. So let's take closer look at each criterion both in greater detail and with a focus on how to make it work for you.

IS IT CURRENTLY FUNCTIONAL?

Here it is useful to return to those shrimp forks that we kept in storage for over twenty years. Safe in their decorative box, the forks clearly remained ready to serve their intended purpose. Yet over the years, we had used our regular forks for any kind of dish involving shrimp. Clearly it meant something that we had never taken these special-use utensils out of the box.

Realistic reflections on our non-use of the shrimp forks helped us face up to the distinction between actual functionality and utility based on "what-if" thinking. Yes, the forks would be entirely functional IF we were setting the table Emily Post style—with three forks and four spoons at each place—and MAYBE we would do this someday. The problem was how to get by the various "ifs" and "maybes" to find the essence of utility.

Current—Versus Theoretical, Past, and Future

It became increasingly clear to us that really functional means CURRENTLY functional—without "ifs" and "maybes" relating to PAST or possible FUTURE uses. Clearly, everything might be considered theoretically functional if we ignored the variables of time and change. IF we lost weight, then those pants or that dress might fit. IF our family ever took its first boating vacation, then we might need those life jackets.

Clothing is a category particularly susceptible to retention simply because it formerly was fashionable or once fit us well. Jill Martin and Dana Ravitch, authors of *I Have Nothing to Wear*, usefully apply the criterion of currently functional to what we retain in our closets. Estimating that most people don't wear 75% of their theoretical wardrobe, they advise being ruthless in weeding out old clothes. The idea is to keep only what makes us look fabulous.[1]

Just as past functionality is no guarantee of present utility, it is important to remember that future functionality also may be an illusion. The seductive question of "what if?" causes our imaginative minds to rescue every sort of thing, no matter how remote its possible future employment. As we thought about our present-day life, we had to let go of those boxes of cancelled postage stamps that we saved for our kids—who never became stamp collectors. Also exiting the premises was that almost-new Ohio snow blower that wasn't going to be helpful given our long-term plans to remain on the California Coast.

No, functionality is not forever. Manufacturers keep improving their products— and having the latest is often a benefit. We were really glad that we unstuffed our '70s harvest-gold crock pot. We replaced it with a sleek, smaller, and oval model that fit much better in our cabinet. And this new crockery, unlike the old one, was dishwasher ready.

Here it is useful to remember that "functional" is a word that begins with "fun." As we toss out that 75% of our closet space devoted to unused duds, we are able to make room for some really fashionable new clothes and accessories. Why not clear the clutter and embrace the joy of looking our best at the start of each season?

A Replacement Budget Based on Savings

Frugality is one of the chief arguments in favor of holding onto things that we used in the past or might use in the future. Yet, as in the case of our improved new crock pot, keeping inventories of obsolescent things may not be truly cost effective in a life lived well. Here it may be more essentially frugal to move along the old and apply the resulting savings to new and better possessions. It's possible to build a tidy replacement budget if we combine monies saved by reducing moving costs, avoiding storage fees, selling on eBay and Craig's List, and factoring in tax deductions—the sum total of our Stuff Cure proceeds.

A replacement budget born of Stuff-Cure savings brings another benefit by alleviating some of the nagging fear that we will make some kind of irredeemable mistake in clearing things out. Of course, the three criteria of functionality, value, and sentiment are powerful protections against regrets. For example, in preparation for our return to California, college-professor Mike reduced his collection of books by about 1,000 when he looked for volumes no longer consulted or that possessed some sales value. So far, he's only missed one of these tomes, and he solved that problem by quickly finding and ordering an inexpensive used copy online. This $6.00 purchase was easily accommodated by our replacement fund.

A bit of research on the Internet gives further reassurance that unstuffing need not result in irretrievable errors. Any of the websites that we list—in Chapter 4—for selling items also represent possible sources for replacements. By this means, we found that gold-plated shrimp forks from the 70s could be easily reacquired; some proved to be of a style more in keeping with our primary tableware.

Hints about Functionality

We recognize that it is often difficult to separate current functionality from its close cousins of theoretical, past, and possible future functionality. So we want to share with you some hints about keeping focus on the idea of CURRENT usefulness. Four questions to ask are these: (1) have you used the item during the last two years? (2) are you waiting for a miracle? (3) do you really require multiples? (4) has it become junk?

The Two-Year Rule. When our eldest son was in the first grade, he was cast in a class play, "Animal University." His part as "The Horse, Of Course" required that his family outfit him with a horse costume complete with hoofs on his hands and horseshoe-type slippers. Betty took on the project with gusto, making an outfit that included a delightful helmet topped with a beautiful mane fabricated from variegated black, gray, and white yarn. Supporting our son's participation in the play became a whole-family activity for several weeks, and we all have great memories of it.

As it came to pass, vestiges of the horse costume remained in the closet for several years afterwards for use in various Halloween get-ups, and Betty also saved the extra yarn in her sewing box. In fact, when our son graduated from college, we realized that we still had the half-skein of yarn from his first-grade costume. At this point we recognized that, if we hadn't used the extra yarn in the intervening 16 years, we would probably never use it. The yarn ended up as a donation to the sewing circle at church.

Keeping the horse-costume yarn for a half a generation supplied one of many experiences that eventually caused us to develop a policy of periodically reviewing stuff for an expiration of functionality. We settled upon two years as the operational measure of "currently functional." If we come upon a stored item that hasn't been used during the last biennium, it becomes a potential candidate for unstuffing.

"Currently" Doesn't Include Miracles. For Mike's twentieth high-school reunion, Betty bought a stunning green dress to wear. It was strapless and quite form-fitting, and Betty told all her friends that she would have won a Best-First-Wife competition in that dress. So for reasons of fashion success, in addition to original expense, Betty kept the outfit in her closet for many years past the time when last she had worn it.

Betty's twentieth-anniversary green dress eventually fell out of her regular wardrobe rotation for the usual reasons. Suffice it to say that, with the passage of years, the outfit no longer flattered. But hope persists, and so this article of clothing kept its spot in the back of the closet. But packing for the thirtieth reunion provided the wake-up call regarding Betty's green dress. She finally had occasion to face the fact that the dress had to go. Only in the movies can a person turn the clock back to earlier decades. With old clothes, miracles rarely happen.

"Currently" Doesn't Include Multiples. Sometimes we acquire multiples of a given functional object either because we use it a lot or because it's hard to find in stores. But most of the time, multiples accumulate as a result of our losing track of what we have. As part of applying the Stuff Cure, we began to pay better attention to what we were keeping on hand. For instance, we discovered that we were in possession of about a dozen nail clippers plus two complete manicure sets. Some of the extras probably resulted from purchases made on various trips or from situations where we had misplaced grooming utensils. Once we got all the clippers in one place, we decided to move along the unnecessary duplicates.

"Currently" Doesn't Include Junk. Is a thing functional at all? Some of our stuff really serves no useful purpose simply because it is old or worn out. Yet we hang on to it for a roster of reasons that amount to the usual suspects of losing track of items stored, lack of time, mistaken thrift, a mania for multiples, wishful thinking, a dash of sentiment.

When Betty was a teenager, her mother was still using bath towels either received as wedding presents or purchased soon after the marriage. These bathroom linens had survived so many washings that they were now threadbare. Betty hated those scratchy, useless old towels, and for her, one of the great treats of travel was the ability to finish a shower with a thick towel. Even though her mother saved the best towels for the guest bathroom, Betty shuddered at the idea that her friends might come upon her family's stock of threadbare linens. Now as an adult Betty makes sure that bathrooms are stocked with luxurious or even oversized towels. She gets new ones whenever the old ones start to become more suitable as rags.

Clearly, the seemingly simple question of "is it currently functional?" is not so simple. Even when we focus on utility, our minds get sidetracked into musings about theoretical, past, and future usefulness. Making the Stuff Cure work is easier if we apply the two-year rule, and if we keep asking ourselves whether false utility waits upon a miracle, is complicated by unneeded multiples, or causes us to become surrounded with junk.

IS IT REALLY VALUABLE?

As we have seen, functionality is difficult to apply because of our excursions into the realms of "what-if" or "maybe when." Fortunately, the second criterion for retaining things is somewhat more straightforward. Real value, we recognize, relates to how much money someone else would be willing to hand us for our stuff.

Isaac had a set of Elgo plastic bricks that he played with as a boy. If the trade name "Elgo" seems strange but yet vaguely familiar, it's because Elgo bricks were a copy of the much more famous and higher quality toys know as Legos. Isaac always thought that his boyhood plastic building-blocks would become valuable because not nearly as many Elgo bricks were manufactured as Legos—and people would want to collect these less-common items.

When Isaac decided to research the value of Elgo bricks, he learned on the Internet that he could buy a set equal to his for about $7.00. This price was probably more that what his parents paid in the 1950s when he was a boy, but in adjusted dollars, probably much less. He had held on to these bulky bricks for years thinking that someday they would become valuable; but that someday never came.

As judged by the marketplace, Isaac's Elgos had only a garage-sale value. But, frankly, it is likely that Isaac's beloved blocks would remain unsold when offered on a driveway card table. So it is not surprising that a charity resale store near us displays a sign by the door that reads "Do not leave garage-sale leftovers on the sidewalk." Clearly, there are many of us who try, and fail, to find a buyer for our cast-off clutter.

Many people raised in the Great Depression of the 1930s learned a survival skill that involved keeping things that they thought might be valuable someday. In our own family, this included a turn-of-the-century treadle sewing machine, an ornate (nonfunctioning) nineteenth-century mantel clock, and some Victorian silver-plate cutlery.

Before the Internet, it was understandable for people to hang onto anything that potentially might be desirable. Owners of antique sewing machines, clocks, and silverware had no real access to information about the market value of stuff. And they, like everyone, had heard tales of someone who bought a picture frame and, voila, found a very old print of the Declaration of Independence behind the faded picture on the front. These stories—the staple of shows like "Antiques Road Show"—tantalize us with a vision of treasures in our attics and cellars.

And it's not just old things that prompt visions of wealth through collecting. In the 1990s, many people were collecting "Beanie Babies." Some of these people rationalized that they were making an investment in this collectable. And in a sense, they were right—provided they had a good sense of timing. Professor I. Nelson Rose explains that "Fortunes really can be made during such wild speculation. You just want to get in and out of the market before the inevitable crash. In other words you want to be the seller of that $5,000 Beanie Baby, not the buyer."[2] And what was the situation after the crash? In November 2010, antiques expert Connie Swaim-Robb reported results from her November 2010 eBay search. She found some 35,787 listings for the Babies, most of which closed with no buyers. Many of these cute stuffed animals, especially those no longer pristine, will end up being donated or trashed.[3]

If you have something that you think might be valuable, we invite you to question whether this object might bring $500 or $1,000. Let's delve more deeply into how we might predict what among your stuff has real dollar value—as measured by the marketplace.

Value Relates to Quality

We like to go to estate auctions. We've observed that, typically, items bringing the highest prices are those that were expensive when originally sold. These include Tiffany lamps, pottery from well-known firms (Roseville, Weller, Rookwood), and fine wood furniture.

Now we are all aware of exceptions to the original-quality rule—such as that first issue of the Superman comic book. Yes, we hear those stories of the dime-store item that originally was cheap but, because of rarity, ended up as something valuable. But more often than not, such stories are both atypical and overstated.

As an example of how cheap usually remains cheap, we have only to think about some 1976 Bicentennial Commemorative 7-Up bottles that we saved for 25 years. When we researched current value, we were not surprised to find that two-and-a-half decades of storage had not transformed these give-away bottles into coveted collector's items. We relegated them to the recycle box.

Value Relates to Scarcity
Some stuff is desirable to collectors because of its status as something hard to find. That first glove worn by Michael Jackson is valuable because it is authentic and one-of-a-kind. But at the end of the day, even a celebrity collectible is worth only what those in the marketplace will pay.

What about a tuxedo shirt that Frank Sinatra owned in 1987? Rick Gorski bought just this item at a garage sale for $5.[4] How much is it really worth? We can speculate endlessly, but the shirt will only sell for what a buyer is willing to pay right now. Better to move the item along—sell or donate—rather than hoping that values will take a big bounce up in the future.

Many times, scarcity is suggested by the term "collector's item." Yet collector's plates are all too commonplace because they are typically produced in issues of thousands or tens of thousands. If you carefully read the ads for these plates, you'll often find that the supposed "collectability" is based on the number of "firing days"—rather than the number of plates actually coming off the line. Once the pottery factory is humming, a lot of plates can be created in just one day. If we enjoy the beauty of a collector's plate, it's a great thing to own. But the resale value, after 10 to 25 years, has usually been less than a dime on the dollar of the original price. These items will never be really valuable because they never were scarce.[5]

Value Relates to Condition
Condition of an object always is key in determining its market value. A few years

ago, some of our friends were excited to read about a Barbie doll that sold for $29,000. Lest we dream that the dolls we played with as children would bring as much, we need to look at the fine print in the story. It turned out that the doll was one of the first originally issued—as proved by its pristine packaging material—and it was in perfect condition. This atypical doll had a hand-painted face and was not one of the mass-produced later models. More than 99% of Barbie dolls are later issues, much played with, and missing the original packaging. They aren't likely to sell for much over a dollar.

Sometimes we can be fooled in matters of an object's condition. "Buyer beware" is a warning well understood by anyone who likes to attend household or estate auctions. Frequently the auctioneer will hold up an item and say, "it looks OK" — meaning that there is no extremely obvious defect. Nevertheless, it behooves a bidder not to put too much reliance on the superficial reassurances of the person holding the gavel. Pottery and china items deserve particularly careful inspection, either before one makes a bid, or IMMEDIATELY after the item is sold (the brief interval when the auctioneer will accept that the buyer didn't cause the damage).

Auctions highlight the real trick of determining condition because estate items mostly are sold "as is"—meaning that the buyer receives no formal appraisal or certified representation of condition. From long experience, we know that the price of pitchers, vases or plates should be strongly discounted if they show chipping (check those rims!), hairline cracks (don't forget to look inside a pot!), fine crazing of the glazed finish, re-glued handles, or other repairs. One or more of these conditions may reduce market value by 50 to 95%.

Sometimes we can be our own worst enemy on matters of condition. We have a friend who was given an original print by the famous French artist, Degas. She wanted to fit her new print into a frame that she already owned, so she trimmed off the sides. Our friend decreased the market value of her artwork by more than half because she damaged its original condition.

If you think that something you own is worth over $1000, and you want to verify your judgment, you can get an independent assessment of value at Value My Stuff *http://www.valuemystuff.com*. You upload pictures of your item and, for a fee, you receive an expert opinion of the value. You may receive additional information that will be useful when you go to sell the item. You can also search eBay *www.ebay.com* for completed listings and see the actual selling price for similar items.

Quality—scarcity—condition. These are three key factors that, when combined with a little Internet research, can help us decide whether our things have significant monetary worth. This is the point at which we can make an informed decision about whether to keep something as a tangible asset—with significant or increasing value—or move the item out of our lives by selling, giving, donating, or trashing it.

IS IT OUTRAGEOUSLY SENTIMENTAL?

But it's not just because of market value that we hold onto things, of course. Sometimes it's for reasons of sentiment. Things sentimental evoke our emotions; these special treasures keep us in contact with the joy of our lives. The first gift from Mike to Betty when they were dating was a toy dancing cat. You wind it up and it waves its arms. It always makes Betty smile.

Betty's dancing cat is neither useful nor valuable; it stays in the family inventory purely because of sentiment. This toy cat falls into the category of OUTRAGEOUSLY sentimental because it represents Mike's first gift to Betty and reflects both his love and sense of humor. What others might see as an ordinary trinket nevertheless uniquely reminds us of that special time when we first fell in love.

For purposes of the Stuff Cure, it's useful to question whether things we own meet the test of unique and special sentimentality. So let's take a closer look at what makes something outrageously sentimental. To start with, exactly what is it that cements an object to our feelings? Seemingly it has to do with memory.

Everything Brings Memories

Our friend, Thelma, was a child of the depression. Born in 1915, Thelma was the seventh of nine children, only six of whom lived to adulthood. Her hardworking family derived adequate sustenance from a hardscrabble farm in western Oklahoma; but there was little cash on hand. Not only did the family have few funds for bric-a-brac or personal luxuries, but as a result of hardship during the Depression, and eventually losing their farm to foreclosure, there were very few possessions of any kind to pass along.

Raised in an environment of thrift and scarcity, Thelma tended to hang on to things throughout her life. And she delighted in picking up small souvenirs—particularly free materials associated with special events that she attended. If there was a name card beside her place at the table, or an identification badge, she was especially proud to keep this record of her name in print.

Not only did Thelma amass a vast collection of paper freebies, but she saved every other kind of trinket distributed at these meetings and conferences—and from her other travels. Most of these calendars, erasers, paperweights, and pens were relegated to drawers, boxes, and closets. The result was an assembly of pleasant reminders—but a mass of things unused, and often becoming unusable.

Thelma herself could never bear to get rid of any kind of memorabilia—because even the humblest paper receipt brought to her mind some pleasant experience with friends or family. Boxes of such minutia accumulated in the basement. Now Thelma was a hardheaded and practical person, so she recognized that eventually she would need to clean out her souvenirs. But when it came to stuff, Thelma's common-sense side never overcame her emotional side.

Many times Thelma's daughter and son tried to help her work through a box or a shelf of old paper or trinkets, but few things ever found their way into the trash can or recycle bin. They were just too memory laden. Only after Thelma died could her family members begin to come to terms with what she had gathered over the years. Few items had any real sentiment for the family—in addition to their lack of utility or marketplace value.

How Precious a Memory?

Thelma's ever-increasing storehouse of mementos highlights the subjectivity of sentiment as a memory trigger. Thelma placed too great a value on the memory triggering aspect of stuff, losing track of the common-sense principle that we can't retain every object that we come into contact with. So one important part of the Stuff Cure is to more efficiently manage our memory triggers.

Here it's helpful for us to ask the simple question of whether something is mildly or outrageously sentimental. Put another way, is every object equally sentimental? Would it be possible to get by with fewer memory triggers?

We ourselves began to apply these questions when we decided to confront our own lifetime legacy of mementos. We discovered that we had saved every card that we received both for our wedding and for the birth of our two sons. Sorting through these cards did remind us of these three particularly happy days. The cards also brought to mind family members and close friends who sent these acknowledgments.

Consistent with the Stuff Cure, we were attempting to apply our common-sense selves to a yard-long file of wedding and birth cards. Because some of the cards contained no handwriting other than signatures, it soon became clear that we really required only a few particularly personalized cards to memorialize these three important events.

And upon further reflection, it became evident to us that two characteristics were in play when something felt outrageously sentimental. The most powerful memory triggers were those that could be characterized as (1) unique and (2) vivid.

The criterion of uniqueness related to our realization that the purpose of memory did not require the overkill represented by stacks of wedding or birth cards. Vividness related to the fact that only a few of the cards contained special hand-written messages from loved ones. Unique and vivid sentiment abided chiefly in a relatively small number of cards. By emphasizing memory triggers that are both unique and vivid, it is possible to reconcile sentiment with a clutter-free life.

In the chapters that follow, we more fully make clear the attitudes and behaviors that, on the one hand, enable us to preserve key memory triggers while, at the same time, maintaining easy access and efficient use of space. But for now, let us point out that it's possible in this electronic age to trigger memory by uploading a few scanned images or photographs. For example, it would be possible to substitute pictures of our grandmother's home instead of squeezing her furniture into our own rooms or storing her decorative plates in the attic or garage.

Pictures made for purposes of memory may be fashioned into remembrance portfolios accessible as a computer link or printed out as a bound volume. Here, a possible wedding portfolio might include a few of the best photos along with such scanned-in items as the pages of the guestbook. Electronic and bound images represent efficient memory triggers because they collect precious thoughts in formats requiring little space and permitting easy access.

The principle underlying the remembrance portfolio is that of creating substitutes for scattered or bulky stuff. Whenever we feel sad or guilty about disposing of mementos, we can fabricate unique and vivid stand-ins in the form of collected images. And we can create verbal substitutes as well. We might develop a paper journal or online blog of memories that are triggered by particular objects that are no longer needed and that are not particularly valuable.

So it is possible, after all, to give a fairly specific answer to the question of "what is a keeper?" When something is currently functional, really valuable, and outrageously sentimental, it passes muster according to the Stuff Cure. On the other hand, when we're not using something on a regular basis, it's not functional—so we can dispose of it. When an item does not amount to a significant long-term asset appreciating in value, we can donate it or extract its small worth by means of a sale. Finally, when something we've retained is not uniquely and vividly meaningful, we can either move it along or replace its sentimentality by means of a memory-triggering portfolio.

When we begin the Stuff Cure, we are like Michelangelo standing before that block of Carrara marble. Poised to create his masterpiece statue of David, he had a vision. But he knew that many chisel strokes would be required before he could display his creation.

WHAT IS A KEEPER?
When It's
Currently Functional,
Really Valuable, *or*
Outrageously Sentimental

In this spirit of Michelangelo—who mixed vision with concrete action—we intend this book to be your guide to a life without clutter. The attitude of wanting just the right stuff— things that are currently functional, really valuable, and/or outrageously sentimental—is the motivational starting point. However, our dreams of uncluttered life come into focus only when we start along a path of simple but very crucial steps. In succeeding chapters, we lay out a proven process for cleansing our drawers, closets, attics, basements, and garages of unneeded, unvaluable, and not particularly sentimental things.

• thestuffcure •

FINDING A BETTER HOME FOR STUFF:
GIFT, SHIFT, AND THRIFT

The Stuff Cure represents a change in our attitude towards material things. Part of this change takes the form of the advice given in Chapter 3. Specifically, it's good to take a hard look at the real functionality and value of what we own; we also would be advised to question whether an item of clutter brings about outrageous sentimentality.

Chapter 4 continues the search for new perspectives on possessions. Under the theme of "finding a better home for stuff," we invite you to consider stuff as essentially transitory—part of the natural processes of change and transformation. Here we consider whether something we're holding onto might be better placed with someone else. Is it possible that things might be moved along in the form of a gift, a shift (a beneficial trade), or a thrifty savings through sale or tax-beneficial donation?

In wrapping our minds around the motivations of gift, shift, and thrift, we'll begin with a story of how one collector used creative gifting to expand her enjoyment of collecting antique china. Our friend, Patience, was known as an avid and successful collector of small cups and other pottery. She was a leading member of a group of china collectors who met regularly—and who often invited expert speakers.

One year, Patience took a creative new approach to trimming her ever-expanding holdings. When hosting the collector's group during the holidays, she assembled a prize table with enough items for everyone. Each of the antique lovers had the opportunity to take home such selections as a Victorian cup and saucer, a footed glass dish, a whimsical salt and pepper shaker set, and a large silver spoon.

What's important from the Stuff-Cure point of view is that Patience had assembled her party prizes entirely from her china surpluses. Operating on the principle of "finding a better home," Patience realized that most of her friends had smaller collections than she; so they could be expected to place a higher value on extras transformed into gifts. This story illustrates one of the fun dimensions of the Stuff Cure—the enjoyment of sharing our stuff-overflow with others who will truly appreciate our generosity.

A BETTER HOME FOR STUFF

The concept of "a better home for stuff" reflects the natural life cycle of things. Some of what we own came from others—and things we now possess will be passed along to new caretakers in the future. A key attitudinal element of the Stuff Cure is to give real and specific attention to that last step in the natural progression of ownership. Here we recognize that our home is not the final repository of things. Further, we recognize that another place for an item may be a better home.

How to recognize a better home? The three related ideas of Gift, Shift, and Thrift can help us wrap our minds around this notion that there may be a new place where our things may be better used or treasured. What we are developing is a new attitude toward what we possess. We make ourselves open to the idea that someone else might find our excess to be more highly functional, more truly valuable, or more outrageously sentimental than we do.

Gift, of course, denotes a transfer of our stuff to those others who will appreciate receiving it—and with no expectation of an exchange. Giving represents altruism because it springs from our generosity and desire to enhance the lives of others.

To shift our stuff differs from gifting in that we pass along things in a reciprocal process. Shifting essentially means trading things by single transaction or through an ongoing process such as a mothers group sharing baby clothes. We pass along something in return for goods or services of approximately equal value.

Thrift takes the form of selling or getting a tax credit for a charitable donation. The objective of thrift, thus, is the most directly commercial outcome of the Stuff Cure. But there's still some higher purpose involved. This is because, rather than hoarding marginal possessions, we participate in a process where others share the benefits of what we have. For instance, people who buy our excess things directly from us or in a second-hand shop usually enjoy a bargain over buying something new.

Let's take a closer look at how we can put these three objectives—gift, shift, and thrift—into practice.

GIFTING WITH A PERSONAL TOUCH

When Mike's cousin, Jane, was installed as a pastor, Mike gave her a bible that had previously been owned by their mutual grandmother. It was a nice leather-bound volume, and it carried sentiment for both of them. But with Jane's new vocation, Mike realized that this family-heritage bible made a perfectly appropriate gift. Mike felt confident that the bible would have the finest possible home in Jane's pastoral study as a volume both useful and sentimental.

More generally, the story of Mike's grandmother's bible illustrates two key principles of moving things along by means of a gift: (1) finding the right person and (2) finding the right occasion

Finding the Right Recipient

Looking for holiday gifts for the office staff, Mike took stock of a collection of sterling silver souvenir spoons inherited from his father. One of the secretaries served as the long-time coordinator of the campus-wide Daffodil Days program of the American Cancer Society. Mike wrapped up a lovely antique spoon for her that was decorated with daffodils. With a bit of ingenuity, Mike was able to find spoons that similarly matched the interests of the other two staff members.

Finding the Right Occasion

As the only daughter in her family, Betty was the intended recipient of a pearl necklace that once had belonged to her grandmother. Because Betty's grandmother died when Betty was a one-year-old, her grandfather gave the pearls to Betty's mother, Lois, for safe keeping. Liking the necklace so much, Lois kept putting off the transfer to Betty, even though she rarely wore this family heirloom during the last 25 years of her life.

Betty finally inherited the pearls when her mother died at age 89. After waiting upon this gift for nearly 40 years, Betty had almost forgotten it. Lois had missed so many meaningful occasions when she could have shared with Betty the mutual joy of gift-giving. Instead, Betty received the necklace only at an age when she had relatively fewer occasions to wear pearls.

What this story suggests is that we should be on the lookout for opportunities to pass along something we treasure to others, such as weddings, graduations, or birthdays. Moreover, we may create our own occasions by means of surprise gifts to special people.

To Surprise a Friend. One Sunday, as Mike's parents, John and Kay, exited their local parish church, Father Bob admired John's brown tweed jacket with natty suede leather patches on the elbows. Having a closet stuffed with nice clothes left over from his working years, John had the jacket dry-cleaned and wrapped it as a gift. He presented it to Father Bob with these words: "Father, I realized that you and I are about the same size, and I thought that you would enjoy having the jacket." When Father Bob later officiated at John's funeral mass, he invoked this story to illustrate John's thoughtfulness and generosity.

To Seize a Moment. When John Sproule passed away, Mike's mother, Kay, took Betty aside and said "I want to show you a box of rings that were given to me as gifts from Johnny. Now that he is gone, I won't be getting out as much, and I want you to accept these rings with all my love." She then brought out a jeweler's display box containing 36 rings, not always expensive, but all amazingly beautiful. Within a year, Kay suffered a seizure that required her to move into a nursing home for round-the-clock attention. On Betty's and Mike's many visits over the next two years, Betty would always wear at least one of the rings. Kay didn't have much to say, but she would always admire whatever jewelry Betty was wearing. When Kay's compliment concerned a ring, Betty would respond by observing "This is one of the rings that you gave me. I am enjoying wearing it." Invariably, Kay would smile and say, "I don't remember ever owning that ring." Kay had timed her gift perfectly.

To Commemorate a Transition. When Mike's mother died, her family included many nieces and nephews who had known her and were sad at her passing. For the next couple of years, when Mike visited one of these cousins, he selected a gift item for them from among Kay's china, glass or jewelry. In each case, he was able to tell a story of how his mother had used or had loved the object

Generous Legacy Versus Re-Gifting

People sometimes worry, quite understandably, about negative connotations associated with gifts known to derive from our store of old things. We've all heard, or seen on the Internet, those urban legends of fruitcakes and cheap champagne passed around for years without ever having been opened. Yet it is easy to distinguish thoughtful and appropriate legacy gifting from the crass re-gifting of castoffs. "Dear Abby" (Jeanne Phillips) explains that re-gifting is no problem "as long as the item is well-chosen for the recipient and is in mint condition."[1] Here we should note that, for antiques and heirlooms, a gift need not be "mint" but should be in desirable form.

Common to John's tweed coat and Kay's rings is the idea of selecting special objects having both personal meaning and good quality. Generous Stuff-Cure gifting always involves the two parties becoming part of a story that links them as family members or in friendship. Stereotypical re-gifting emanates from an ungenerous seizing upon unwanted objects as quick-and-dirty substitutes for a true gift. We find, here, a distinct absence of either quality or any unifying story of family or friendship.

Try taking the following test to be sure that you are proceeding along the lines of Stuff-Cure legacy gifting rather than mere re-gifting. Ask yourself:

1) Is the gift especially appropriate for the recipient? [Ideally, YES.]
2) Is there a personal story associated with the gift? Does the story link giver and recipient? [Ideally, YES and YES.]
3) Does the gift possess quality, utility, or sentiment? [Ideally, YES.]
4) Will the gift be as much or more welcomed than something you've found new in a store? [Ideally, YES.]
5) Are we gifting something we ourselves don't value? or that has recently been received from someone else? [Ideally, NO and NO.]

SHIFTING BY TRADING

Before money existed, people traded things. And because cash is always in short supply—combined with the fact that our needs and tastes change—barter has continued as a common practice. We own things that others want more than we do—and vice versa. All these ideas suggest that trading can be an important part of the Stuff Cure. Sometimes all it takes is a bit of creative thinking, together with some practical negotiation, to find the win–win in an exchange.

Trading with Friends

When we were expecting our first baby, one of our friends invited us to connect with a mothers cooperative that exchanged baby clothes. We now enjoyed instant access to a good wardrobe. Furthermore, the previously worn and washed items were not as stiff as new clothes.

Dealing with clothes outgrown and toys no longer played with gives parents a natural introduction to wider practice of trading. It's not just for kids' stuff. We picked up an answering machine in exchange for our old baby stroller. Emilie Hyams of Manhattan organized her friends for a swap of suits and purses. She served wine and cheese and had quite a festive event. Each invitee brought clothes to swap and agreed to make a $10 donation to a local battered women's shelter. Any clothes that were not claimed by participants also went to the shelter. She used Swap for Good *www.SwapforGood.org* to organize the event.[2]

Sharing with friends can be a fun way to minimize surplus or obsolete stuff in our lives, while at the same time, meeting new needs without spending money. Stuff-Cure trading, particularly where we work together with friends in a party atmosphere, represents a longstanding tradition in the U.S. Here we are updating the quilting bees and barn raisings of yesteryear.

Internet Swapping

The Internet has proved to be more than simply an alternative to shopping in a store. Online activity greatly facilitates the creative reuse of stuff either for free or by means of trade. Further, unlike garage sales or swap meets, the Internet brings the marketplace into our own homes. And Internet trading also removes the awkwardness of bargaining with people we know.

Internet trading and bartering became increasingly popular with the Great Recession of 2008 that motivated people to find ways to conserve money and get the best use out of their existing stuff. People searched out websites designed to facilitate the swapping of things and services. Swap It Now *www.Swap-It-Now.com* started as a site for people who wanted to trade DVDs. Such sites can be quite popular, as in the case of Swap Thing *www.SwapThing.com* with its 162,000 members who have found an everyday a bazaar for goods and services. The well-known Craig's List *www.Craigslist.com* has a category for bartering. Similar websites include Trade a Favor *www.TradeaFavor.com,* Joe Barter *www.JoeBarter.com*, Swap *www.swap.com,* and Swap Mamas *www.swapmamas.com.*

Trading children's clothes has its own site at Thred Up *www.ThredUP.com.* Members package 15 "new to you" items in a box and then list the contents of the box on the site by size, brand, gender, and style. Other participants can purchase the box for $5 plus the cost of shipping. Everyone contributes boxes of their own as part of participating in the network. Additional sites for swapping baby gear include Swap Baby Goods *www.swapbaby-goods.com* and Zwaggle *www. Zwaggle.com.*[3]

Shifting enables us to find a better home for some of our stuff without any exchange of cash. Sometimes, however, the marketplace permits us to receive cash or credit in exchange for our old things. Moreover, many high-value items—such as cars, antiques, and jewelry—can be used as a trade-in when you purchase an item of higher value.

If you anticipate that money will become involved in an exchange of goods, you will want to seek out advance information about the value, condition, and scarcity of the item you are passing along. Knowledge always enhances our competence in executing a trade that maximizes benefits. Generally, the more valuable is the object you wish to trade, the more options and negotiating power you will have. We'll elaborate further on this point in a following chapter section dealing with sales. However, it is worth mentioning at this point that the Internal Revenue Service considers income from bartering to be part of our gross taxable income. You will want to keep records to show that any value received from barter is offset by the initial value of what you traded. One owes taxes only on net gains from an exchange.

THRIFT THROUGH DONATION

A counterpart to giving and trading is donation. Donation is ideal for those situations when our excess or obsolescent things seem unsuited for easy redistribution among friends. An item might be too specialized to suit anyone in our circle. Maybe something needs a bit of repair. Maybe the quality is somewhat less than the ideal. Yet our sense of thrift, or concern for the planet, nags at our conscience, prompting us to seek a venue nobler than the garbage dump. Let's take a closer look at donation as a creative element of the Stuff Cure.

It's appropriate to begin with a worst-case scenario—something bulky, of low value, or of highly specialized use. Hard-to-dispose-of objects may be distinguished from easily usable firewood or clean lumber, the both of which disappear quickly when put out on the curb under a sign marked "free." In contrast, such more problematic potential reusables as a toilet tank—even when still in original box—are unlikely to be picked up at random. Yet even these items are suitable for your town's annual Pick-Up-Anything Day. Be on the lookout for announcements of dates when the local trash service will scoop up whatever is put out on the curb. But be sure to read the fine print; otherwise you will find some of your curbside castoffs remaining there at the end of the day. Hazardous chemicals, for example, may be disposable only at the community recycling center.

Curbside donation has its place, but those versed in the Stuff Cure use it as only a last resort. Before you put things out next to the street, you will want to review the other alternatives offered in this book. Because our family has made a habit of systematically donating useful items, we are often amazed at what people put out as trash. Many times we've seen castoff chairs, tables or file cabinets in very usable condition—or ready for easy repair or refinishing. So it's common to find pickup trucks circling through neighborhoods at the crack of dawn to load up useable— even valuable—items before the city collection trucks arrive.

As you assimilate the lessons of the Stuff Cure, you'll come to appreciate what the pickup-truck drivers and dumpster divers already know, namely that donating represents a Triple Threat—gift, shift, and thrift! And it's not that difficult.

Donating to a General Agency

Do you commonly itemize deductions for your federal or state income tax? If so, it is important to remember that non-cash donations—as well as dollar contributions—may be used to reduce your taxable income. Of course, you'll need to keep records and receipts as well as making sure that you are donating to a nonprofit agency registered with the IRS as a 501 (c) 3 organization. Check the website for this information.

You may do a search—yellow pages, smart phone, computer—to find agencies in your community that are qualified to accept tax-deductible goods. General agencies, such as Goodwill *www.goodwill.org* and the Society of St. Vincent de Paul, Inc. *www.svdpusa.org*, very happily receive useable clothes, household goods, and other items of value. These organizations process your castoffs, not only providing useful employment for many people but also showcasing low-priced goods in their stores. The websites of these organizations usually indicate the types of things acceptable. But you may also consult the website Donate Things *www.donatethings.com* not only for the names of 501 (c) 3 organizations in your area but also for the particulars concerning these agencies. Again, we emphasize that you should anticipate donating only useable merchandise in good and clean condition.

Many charitable organizations contact neighborhood addresses in advance to alert people that used items may be left on the curbside at a particular time. In addition, some charities will send a truck directly to your home if you contact them about a large donation or if you are disposing of furniture or other large items.

Tax authorities are well aware of the natural human tendency to overvalue our possessions, so you will need to pay particular attention to record keeping. Of course, you will want to ask for a receipt. But you should know that most charitable organizations will not take the responsibility of placing a value on items donated. Usually they will offer you a printed form with space for you to list items and estimated values. However, agencies often provide a sample table of values for categories of items sold in their stores. In any event, be sure to use thrift-store pricing in estimating non-cash contributions at tax time. The IRS asks taxpayers to separately list any item or collection of items valued at more than $500.

Specialized Donating

Occasionally, you will find an organization whose mission fits the items you wish to donate. Most of us are familiar with the fact that libraries typically raise funds through sales of donated books. But a bit of looking around will reveal other such opportunities to place our excess things with specialized charitable agencies.

For example, Bike Works in St. Louis, Missouri *www.bworks.org* accepts donations of bicycles and bicycle parts. Bike Works uses these parts to refit two-wheelers for kids who have no other opportunities. Volunteers do the repairs and match bikes to their recipients.

A number of organizations specialize in good-quality stuffed animals. Stuffed Animals for Emergencies *http://www.stuffedanimalsforemergencies.org/How_to_ Donate.html* is an organization that provides police, fire, and rescue personnel with animals for distribution to children who are in distress. Adopt a Platoon *http:// adoptaplatoon.org/site/?page_id=259* provide gifts for U.S. deployed troops to distribute in their humanitarian missions. Loving Hugs *http://www.lovinghugs.org/* distributes stuffed animals throughout the world to people in need.

Got shoes? Soles4Souls *www.soles4souls.org* takes your donations of gently used shoes to redistribute to people in need around the world. Eyeglasses? The Lions Club *www.lionsclubs.org* collects used glasses at Wal-Mart stores and other locations for redistribution to people who need eyewear. You can find more about this program, as well as a location near you, at the website.

Higher-End Donating

In some cases, we find ourselves wanting to dispose items having far more than thrift-shop value. Of course, these would be candidates for sale or auction, but it also may be possible to turn such better-quality disposables into a significant contribution. An example would be donating antiques to the Little Shop around the Corner, a fund-raising arm of the Missouri Botanical Gardens. Consistent with how such higher-value items typically are treated, staff members of the Little Shop present the donor with a formal appraisal for tax purposes. We ourselves used this approach to quickly and efficiently unstuff some lovely glassware and furniture in preparation for our transcontinental move.

It's likely that you'll be able to find some high-value donating opportunities in your neck of the woods. Folks in the San Francisco Bay Area of California are aware of the semiannual Stanford Treasure Market. Every two years, volunteers in Palo Alto, California host this event that raises money for the university art program. Volunteer appraisers provide a receipt to donors. The event grew out of Stanford's practice of de-accessing various art pieces to raise funds for new ones.

Even folks who don't have much art can find themselves needing to dispose of a still-usable automobile. Accordingly, you will find notices in the media about organizations that solicit your donation of a car that they can sell to raise funds. Be sure that you are donating your car to a credible organization that is prepared

(1) to give you a detailed receipt of estimated value and (2) has a procedure for documenting the transfer of title. You'll need a credible receipt for the IRS in the case of any high-value donation, and you'll need a release of ownership to absolve you of any further legal responsibility for the vehicle.

The idea of high-valued donating always makes us reflect back on our friend, Christopher, who liked collecting antique yard sticks. Christopher greatly enjoyed showing his friends the advertising and other logos on these quaint reminders of daily life in a simpler time. One of his prizes, a stick that touted The New Paris (Ohio) Lumber Company, invited customers to call them at phone number "15." Chris eventually amassed a collection of over 1,500 of these measuring instruments, but eventually realized that he needed to dispose of the collection as part of his move into smaller post-retirement housing.

Saving a dozen or so of the best yardsticks for himself, Chris donated the remaining 1,495 to the local historical society. The society raised money by selling the yardsticks for between $1 and $5 in their gift shop. The society verified the donation, signing off on a professional estimate of value that Chris had secured from a local auctioneer.

Free-Cycling

Long before the Internet, our neighbor, Nathan, occasionally put stuff out at his curb with a sign marked "Free." Having a good hunch for what people would want, Nathan's stuff was always gone by morning. From a growing awareness of the need to reuse and recycle, this practice now goes by the name "Free-Cycling."

Websites such as Free Stuff *www.freestuff.com* and Free Cycle *www.freecycle.com* enable you to list things that others might want as freebies. Provided you don't care about the cash or the tax deduction, free-cycling is a great way to downsize a garage or an attic.

Tips for Donating

Even if you aren't in a position to itemize non-cash donations for tax purposes, donation still brings benefits. First, from the Stuff-Cure perspective, it permits quick dispersal of excess things. Second, you are in a position to make the world just a bit better by supporting the mission of the receiving organization or agency.

Consistent with the social benefits of donation, our local Goodwill trucks sport the catchphrase, "We change people's lives."

If you will be itemizing non-cash contributions for tax purposes, you will find it helpful to consult relevant Internal Revenue Service and state tax agency guidelines. IRS publication 526 *http://www.irs.gov/pub/irs-pdf/p526. pdf* is particularly useful. In addition, Turbo Tax offers a free online tool *https:// itsdeductibleonline.intuit.com* to facilitate keeping track of both cash and non-cash donations. For in-kind donations, they provide an estimate of value for comparable items based on selling prices from eBay. Turbo Tax also provides updates based on current tax law concerning deductions for donations.

Sometimes it's possible to do a bit of pre-donation homework to check whether your goods are acceptable either in general or with respect to the mission of the intended recipient. You may consult the government website on recalls *www. recalls.gov* to find if your item is entered on the list of products recalled by the manufacturer—more than 300 products are recalled each year.[4] No agency wants recalled items. You can always call an agency directly to inquire whether they will accept a specific item.

THRIFT THROUGH SELLING

Systematic donating has yet to become as American as apple pie. But nearly everyone is familiar with the garage sale, the flea market, and the community swap meet. And eBay *www.eBay.com*, as well as similar but more specialized websites, always are a click away whenever we think about selling our stuff.

In this section, our focus is picking up some extra cash by selling our stuff at garage sales, consignment sales, estate sales, and on the Internet. Although all of these sales venues are aimed at the same result, you may find that you enjoy one more than another or that factors of time or process management will influence your choice of how to sell.

One basic fact to keep in mind is that even if our excess stuff is in its original package, buyers will regard it as "used." So we're going to lose that premium that comes with "brand new," and our customers will be focused on saving money. We need to focus less on getting "top dollar" and more on quickly and efficiently picking up a quick bonus of some extra cash.

Garage Sales

When we lived in Texas, our neighbor, Morgan, loved to host garage sales to fund her annual trip to Las Vegas. Nothing in her house was too small or too valueless to escape her keen eye for potential sales items. Her sales patter was good, also, and we recall once picking up a small box of empty glass jars, helped along by her encouraging ideas about making jelly from our backyard fruit trees. The jars were washed, well packaged for transport, and seemed a bargain package.

If you enjoy meeting the local bargain hunters who frequent garage and neighborhood sales, Morgan's method of selling will be fun for you. Follow her technique of attractively displaying clean items with prices clearly marked. Be ready to deal even before the posted time on your ad; bargain-hunters often skim several sales early to be sure of getting the best selection.

Sometimes community associations, or several households on a block, organize a neighborhood sale. If you decide to step up and initiate something of this kind, you'll enjoy the added benefit of meeting your neighbors. Our association of homes in south Palo Alto, California, periodically arranged for just such an event that took place in the small park next to the community pool. We used the occasion to set up a table on which we displayed some used books, a few antique 78 jazz records, children's toys, and some household equipment.

Many garage sale organizers arrange for a local charity to come at the end of the sales day and pick up useable yet unsold goods. Anything that the charity does not want may be consigned responsibly to the trash. Look for tips about successful garage-sale events at sites such as Allied Van Lines *http://www.allied.com/moving-tips/garage-sales.aspx* or Yard Sale Queen *http://www.yardsalequeen.com/.*

The bottom line, of course, is this: Sell stuff that people want, and be prepared to negotiate. Remember that a rack of shabby and unfresh adult clothes will remain on premises at the end of the day. In contrast, clean children's clothing of good quality will be snapped up quickly. And be sure to remove in advance any chip on your shoulder relating to your goods. People are likely to make tacky remarks, partly because they think it will help reduce the price. Be patient even when dealing with what seems a ridiculous request—as when one of our buyers brought back a disposable end table (consisting of circular plastic top with paper sides) that we had priced at a dollar. Her beef was that the top wasn't teak wood. Teak for a dollar? Can't distinguish wood from plastic and paper? Well, we took it back, anyway, and resold it fairly soon thereafter.

Flea Markets

Flea Markets are booming across the U.S. in these days when people are particularly attuned to bargain prices. Some shoppers go for the thrill of the hunt and the opportunity to sort through the detritus of yesteryear to find something unique and especially meaningful, such as a favorite childhood book. Other shoppers go for just for the savings. Still others enjoy the atmosphere of congeniality brought about by the noise of the crowd, the food carts, and the friendly vendors.[5]

There are some things to remember, though, when you consider transitioning from customer to vendor. You may find it necessary to secure a vendor's license or sales permit, and there may be other up-front costs. Possibly your objectives may be served by finding a vendor who will sell some of your stuff on consignment.

Selling on the Internet

For computer and technology buffs, selling stuff on the Internet has become a useful, profitable, and fun activity. Internet selling is particularly sales efficient because it attracts a wider range of potential customers as compared to the crowd that might drop by your garage or neighborhood. You can find sales opportunities at sites like eBay *www.eBay.com*, Craig's List *www.CraigsList.org*, and Amazon *www. Amazon.com*. Portero *www.portero.com* specializes in selling pre-owned luxury goods. There are also Internet sites for the classified ads in your local newspaper.

The websites listed above typically provide instructions describing what constitutes good seller behavior. Be sure to educate yourself on how the process works because stuff on the Internet has a way of coming back at you. Making early mistakes can earn you a bad vendor rating.

As an example of becoming an effective Internet vendor, let's take the example of selling Roseville pottery on eBay—something that happens every day. Experienced sellers know to use the exact item descriptions and numbers taken from original Roseville catalogues. Precision brings the best price because collectors search for exactly the pieces they need. In addition, having a reasonable market price—based on past sales—and taking attractive pictures helps bring the best sales results. Because any kind of pottery is likely to have a defect or two—chips at the rim, handles re-glued, or crazing (fine superficial cracks) on the finish—you will help along your sales and vendor rating by representing these defects accurately in commentary or in pictures.

After the sale comes delivery. Vendors customarily include a stated shipping charge as part of the purchase price. Be prepared to pack and ship the item within two days after sale. If you don't want the hassle of listing and shipping items on your own, you can use the services of an online trading assistant. Find one near your home at eBay Trading Assistant *http://ebaytradingassistant.com*. These services either charge a fee and/or take a percentage of the sales price.

Books seem an especially promising category for online sales not only because everyone has them, but also because they are easy to ship without risk of damage. It's also easy to set a realistic price by checking Amazon *www.amazon.com* or more specialized sites such as Bookfinder *www.bookfinder.com* or AbeBooks *www.abebooks. com*.

You will find that it's not difficult to use a book's ISBN number to list it for sale at Powell's Books *www.powells.com/sellonline*, Half Price Books *http://www.hpb.com/ selltous*, or Amazon *www.amazon.com*. If you have a large quantity of books, and you want someone else to handle the task for you, Resale Solutions *www.resale-solutions.biz* deals with millions of books each year. They'll pick up books, sell those of value, and share the proceeds with you—and they'll save you the trouble of donating or recycling the remainder.

Cell phones and other electronic devises also present particularly favorable opportunities for selling on the Internet. Capstone Wireless *www.capstonewirelessllc. com* buys back all varieties of cell phones, as long as they power up and have a good LCD display. Gazelle *www.gazelle.com* buys more than 20 categories of electronics. Apple offers a gift card in exchange for reusable Apple computers *www.apple.com/recycling/*.

Consignment Selling

Consignment shops represent a great way to save money on stuff that you will need for only a limited time. Parents of babies and small children often frequent consignment shops where slightly used equipment and clothes are sold. The

National Association of Resale and Thrift Shops reports that net sales in thrift shops were up 13% in 2010 compared to 2009, the strongest growth in five years.[6]

Consignment buyers often return as sellers. Because consignment merchants typically know much more about the marketability of goods than you do, their value-added pricing may increase your net return. Expect to pay a fee, usually 25% to 50% of the sales price, to market your stuff via a consignment seller whose fee covers preparation, display, shipping, and sales-tax collection.

To find a resale shop in your area check the National Association of Resale and Thrift Shops *www.narts.org* to search for stores based on your zip code or city.

Pawn Shops

Pawn shops emerged over 3,000 years ago in China. Yet the idea is so fresh in the current millennium that "Pawn Stars" is a popular TV show. Then as now, the pawn broker provides you with a loan in exchange for holding your things as collateral. For example, Pioneer Loan and Jewelry in Las Vegas fronts a customer up to 80% of what they determine to be an item's value, with a further catch that they are free to sell it after 120 days. Owners can reclaim their possessions within the 120-day period by repaying the loan plus 10 percent interest for every 30 days.[7] To find a pawn shop near you, check Pawn Shops *www.pawnshops.net*.

If your intention is to dispose of something permanently, rather than retrieve it later, pawn shops are probably not your best choice for unstuffing. You won't want to pay the premium they charge. On the other hand, an occasional visit to a pawn shop provides valuable Stuff-Cure lessons. You'll get a great reminder of what people are willing to part with when the need arises.

Auctions

J.R. Ewing—the charming villain played by Larry Hagman in "Dallas"—captured the imagination of many TV viewers with his affluence and lavish lifestyle. Some years after the show went off the air, Hagman commented that "There comes a time, even in J.R. Ewing's life, when you have to downsize."[8] His auction of memorabilia took place on June 4, 2011. You can see the list of the 413 items sold, together with amounts paid, at Julien's Auctions *http://www.juliensauctions. com/auctions/2011/larry-hagman/results.html*. We would expect that Hagman's stuff brought a premium for having been owned previously by a famous person. Nevertheless his results remind us that it is rare for an auction to return but a fraction of an item's original cost.

Yet auctions are so much a part of American culture that you will find them happening every week in your community. On a regional or national level, auctions for high-value items are so familiar a part of the world of art and design that many major auction houses have been in business for over 100 years. You can check out the scene for yourself at Christies *www.Christies.com*, Sotheby's *www. sothebys.com*, Bonhams & Butterfields *www.bonhams.com*, and Ivey Selkirk *www. ivyselkirk.com*.

Estate Sales

When her mother died, our friend Merlyn was named the executor of the estate, a task that involved disposing of a considerable amount of household property. Merlyn and her two brothers took turns choosing items from the estate, with the understanding that the rest would be sold at a public estate auction. As it turned out, Merlyn's estate auction proved useful in resolving one further problem, namely that of her two brothers both wanted a Chagall print depicting the ceiling of the Paris Opera House. They each got half the cash instead.

You can locate an estate-sale provider in your area by checking Estate Sales *www. estatesales.net*. This option proved to be so popular that this particular site boasts of having doubled its business every year from 2005 to 2010. In December 2010, Estate Sales listed an average of 75,000 sales per week with more than 150,000 people signed up to receive email alerts.[9]

Some Tips on Selling

When selling your unwanted stuff for cash, you want to get the maximum return for the least effort expended. But when you enter the marketplace, it helps to begin looking at things from the point of view of the customer. Business people call this market research, and its principles are applicable to small-scale sellers as well. You'll need to consider the desirability and quality of your items as well as what buyers would consider a reasonable price.

Be Realistic about Your Stuff. Your potential customers typically are searching for lightly used goods or antiques. Be sure to represent accurately the goods you are trying to sell. Be objective in describing any nicks or scratches that lower the usability or appearance.

Value Pricing. In this age of the Internet, it's likely that your buyers are as knowledgeable as you with regard either to current prices being asked for or the results of past sales and auctions. The price you paid for an object has very little bearing on the amount that others would regard as a fair market price. As a rule of thumb, it is well to price most items at no more than 20% of store prices, even if gently used. Clothing should be priced at 10% or less of its original price. Anything of substantial value—cars, antiques, and jewelry—should be priced at a condition-calibrated value based on your research of Internet sites.

The Occasional Surprise. Once in a while, something will actually sell for more than you paid for it. One of our California friends experienced this serendipity when disposing of a hybrid automobile. Her sale occurred during a brief window of opportunity when owners of hybrid vehicles possessing a limited-issue sticker enjoyed the privilege of driving in carpool (High Occupancy Vehicle) lanes. A couple of years later, owners of these vehicles no longer enjoyed the premium sales value brought by a limited-time carpool sticker.

KEEP REPEATING:
Stuff doesn't last forever.
We are stuff guardians for only a time.
Stuff is subject to natural change
and transformation.

AN ATTITUDE ABOUT STUFF FOR OUR FUTURE

We've ended on the notion of getting money for excess things. So is useful to return to the key idea of this chapter, namely, that the Stuff Cure represents a change in attitude about possessions. Sure, it's nice on occasion to convert unneeded objects into cash; yet the basic idea is broader. The Cure is less about what we can get and more about paring away the nonessentials. We're hoping that you will take to heart our mantra of "gift, shift, and thrift."

This mantra of the Unstuffed Life represents a journey in which people focus less on good things and more on good stewardship. Here we think about what is essential in life. Home may be where the heart resides; but stuff can be transitioned. As we search for new and better locations for our stuff, we attend to our small place in the larger created world to which humanity has been given only a temporary title. Hallmarks of this life of stewardship include the generosity of giving, the community spirit that comes with trading, and the environmentally astute reuse of things. In Chapter 5, we elaborate further on this idea of stewardship as the basis of our stuff life.

• thestuffcure •

STEWARDSHIP OF STUFF:
THE SEVEN MORPHS

When our friend, Mary, returned from the hospital for some at-home
recuperation, we wanted to show our concern; so we sent her a dozen DVDs from
our collection. We culled these lighthearted selections from our roster of over
800 discs as part of our new attitude toward this accumulation. Our old approach
had been that of the Library of Congress, where acquisitions are permanent. But
we now were applying the gift-shift-thrift attitude outlined in Chapter 4. In this
spirit, Mary's living room DVD player represented "a better home" for a few of
our movies.

The activities of gift, shift, and thrift all serve as triggers for periodic unstuffing.
But they do not, in themselves, offer a complete blueprint for living the Unstuffed
Life. The good stewardship of all things material requires that we embrace a
soup-to-nuts treatment of our possessions. This approach begins when we restrain
our urge to consume, and it continues through that last resort of the Stuff Cure,
namely, the trash bin. But as we become more astute as stewards, we find ourselves
less frequently consigning castoffs to the ashcan and more often extending their
functionality through reuse or recycling.

With apologies to Snow White and her friends, we have appropriated "Seven
Morphs" as a designator for the good stewardship of stuff; this because the word
"morph" denotes changing the form of a thing. The responsible stewardship part
of the Stuff Cure is all about transforming overflowing or long-stored possessions
into something better—better used, better valued, and better cared for. Here we
have in mind the biblical story of the Good Steward who won praise for doing
the best that was possible with resources given him by the master.

In the example of Mary's new DVDs, we understood "better" to mean finding
someone who would appreciate the discs even more than we did. But responsible
stewards do more than find an occasional delighted new owner for the unneeded
or unused. More broadly, these stewards take as an objective to live life with

lessened impact on Mother Earth. With seven billion people already on the planet, good stewards aim for a less material-centered life in the mode of Jesus, Buddha, Saint Francis of Assisi, Mohammed, and Gandhi.

> # The Basic 3 R's
> ## Reduce
> ## Reuse
> ## Recycle

Environmentalists often refer to the three R's of reducing, reusing, and recycling as strategies for minimizing one's planetary footprint. To fully implement the stewardship aspect of the Stuff Cure, we've beefed up this list to arrive at the Seven Morphs of unstuffing. They are these:

> *refraining*
> *restraining*
> *returning*
> *reusing*
> *renting*
> *recycling*
> *and*
> *rendering into trash*

Below, we present each Morph with details and examples about putting the technique into practice. We hope the first six Morphs will inspire your creativity about getting rid of stuff; that way, your stewardship may go beyond that seventh Morph of rendering into trash.

REFRAINING

Refraining means to never acquire stuff in the first place. All too often when we look at some of our stuff we think, "Why did I ever buy that?" We may have acquired it in a moment of impulse or at a sale we couldn't resist. Sometimes a trinket was free or was an advertising gimmick. We may have saved money by getting something "on sale" or even "free"; but there are hidden costs to keeping that stuff in our life.

The Price of "Free"

It's not unusual to find tabletops, drawers, and closets filling up with clutter gotten for free. Grocery-store trips produce extra plastic bags and twisty ties. Rubber bands accumulate from newspapers and the mail. Shirts return from the laundry with a fistful of hangers. Perfume samples fall out of magazines. Everyday these freebies settle into our homes like dust wafting onto a table.

And a lot of this free stuff stays around such that, slowly but surely, we accumulate burdens by hanging on to it. Consider the free samples that accompany purchases of cosmetics. Possibly we will use these extras as helpful additions to our travel kit. But it's more likely that, since we didn't pick out these complementary items, we find them a bit "off." The scent may be wrong or the shade of lipstick or foundation may be unflattering. Possibly the product contains chemicals that we're allergic to. All in all, it's highly likely that we'll lay aside these freebies in hopes of some possible future use. But it's more likely that they will only be forgotten at the back of the drawer. Better never to have received these samples; better to have given them away immediately; better to have saved our prime storage real estate for things we actually want and use.

Cosmetics represent just one instance of "the tyranny of the free." The same principle applies to our accumulations of cheap plastic cups and water bottles. There's a cost in terms of storage and frustration that comes with the false thriftiness of hanging onto things that we'll never employ.

Following are some ideas for heading off "the tyranny of the free."

Pre-Cycling—Getting Off the Lists

From today, begin to take your name off mailing lists; and stop subscribing to magazines, newspapers, and catalogs you never read. The Direct Marketing Association *www.the-dma.org* has a website with a service to remove names from many mailing lists. The government has a do-not-call website *www.donotcall.gov* so you don't get unsolicited phone calls. You can write the firm and request to "take me off." You can also write "refused" on envelopes received, and the post office will return to the sender.

Planet Green has a term for these activities—pre-cycling. By never receiving the material in the first place, you have achieved the ultimate efficiency in downsizing.

Check out Planet Green *www.planetgreen.com/precycle* for more information about services available to help cut down what you receive.

Worried that pre-cycling will cause you to miss out on vital information? In today's world of websites and email options, it's ever easier to get information just in time. So feel free to get off distribution lists whenever updated or new information no longer interests you. You can apply the same principle to your household record keeping. Many accounts—utilities, banks, mortgage, and even trash pick-up—give you an option to manage your account without receiving printed statements.

The trend toward just-in-time information—as opposed to an endless onslaught of paper—continues unabated. The U.S. Postal Service 10-K Annual Report states that, nationally, the volume of mail has been reduced, coinciding with the availability of non-print alternatives. Mail volume fell by 6.2 billion pieces in 2010 and by 26.0 billion pieces in 2009. The migration to electronic media accelerated during the Great Recession of 2008, and the Postal Service expects this trend to continue.[1]

Don't get us wrong, print has its place for the important stuff—marriage licenses, deeds, and the like. And print remains the most reliable form of long-term storage; just try finding a computer to read those old floppy disks! But in this electronic era, there's no longer a reason to keep boxes of maps, and the like.

RESTRAINING

Even if we can't "just say no," then we can reduce by means of restraint. Here the idea is simply to minimize the amount of new stuff we accept. Our mental attitude is that of "Just a little, please."

Now, there can be a time for buying in bulk—for instance, to make sure that enough diapers always are on hand, along with soap and toilet paper for a big family. But when the household consists of but two adults, it's safe to reduce the amount of disposable items in storage. Also, it's possible to replace disposables with reusables. Some people prefer cloth napkins and towels to their paper equivalents.

Here are some strategies to avoid buying too much.

Fewer Dustables

Our friend, Audrey, uses the term "dustables" for knickknacks that look cute and sit on a shelf or table. Audrey is a sucker for little pottery souvenirs, and so she has to watch herself so to avoid buying too many of these dustables—because she doesn't enjoy dusting. When out and about, Audrey keeps repeating to herself, "Is it really just a dustable?"

Dustables represent a category that, in the Stuff-Cure mindset, always is a good target for review. Think of it this way: When you are tempted to box up the dustables, maybe that's the time to move them out of your life instead of into the garage or attic.

Fewer Vacation Baubles

When on vacation, most of us feel compelled to pick up things in the belief that we may never be back. As we look for reminders of a fun excursion, souvenirs sometimes begin to fall into the category of things sentimental.

Yet vacation accoutrements can look pretty tacky when taken from their natural context—such as that dried baby alligator. Similarly, a local logo may begin to detract from the beauty of a cedar box. In addition, in this age of Internet shopping for both new and used goods, why pay the tourist's premium?

Bottom line: If you want memories from your trip, we recommend that you take lots of pictures.

Fewer Clothes

Fashion is fun. But from a Stuff-Cure perspective, it's important to stick to the basics and to move along the out-of-date. Bravo TV's Tim Gunn in "Tim Gunn's Guide to Style Wardrobe Room" *http://www.bravotv.com/tim-gunns-guide-to-style/ games/tim-gunns-guide-to-style-wardrobe-room* gives us an idea of basic fashion in his standard shopping list for clothes. Gunn's outline of the fundamentals includes the following functional foundation for any woman's wardrobe:

1. Basic black dress
2. Trench coat
3. Dress pants

4. Classic shirt

5. Jeans

6. Any occasion top

7. Skirt

8. Day dress

9. Jacket

10. Sweat suit alternative

11. A bonus of one indulgent trendy item

If we keep our wardrobe closer to these essentials, we will find ourselves with a great deal more closet space—to say nothing of more cash on hand.

And fashion is not forever. Style consultants remind us that clothes typically go out of date, or are generally less flattering, after about three years. It's good to review what's older than three years and what hasn't been worn in the past 365 days.

We're reminded, here, of Mike's vintage 1975 sport coat. With its fabric of bright yellow, green, white, and blue plaid—complemented with dark blue ultra-suede accents—this garment represented fashion excellence in the era of Austin Powers. "Yeah, Baby!" Even though Mike stopped wearing it, the jacket remained in the closet through the 90s. We realized that we had kept it too long when one of our sons, then in high school, asked his dad if he could wear the coat as a hilarious costume for a 70s theme day at school.

Resources for Restraint

Some people buy clothes; others download apps with abandon. Whatever is the focus of your spending passion, it's possible to keep things in control as part of the Stuff Cure. Budgeting and record keeping become crucial.

Brain scientists are beginning to research why some people spend with abandon and others are savers. They've discovered measurable differences when the brain is focused on acquiring versus conserving. Results further show that even children can be trained to recognize that forgoing pleasure now can bring a greater payoff later. Paul Zak of Claremont Graduate University emphasizes that anyone can develop willpower and patience through practice.[2]

A good way to begin is by making a budget that includes your major stuff temptations. That way, if you want to go over on one category of the budget, then you have to restrain yourself somewhere else. Betty learned an early lesson in this kind of budgeting when, still living with her parents, she received her first big post-college paycheck. Her father insisted that Betty save part of the money and make a budget for how she would spend the rest. He suggested that she change her spending money into one dollar bills (this was the 1970s). This all-cash approach created a natural restraining effect. When Betty bought something, she had to count out the number of bills required. This exercise created a vivid impression that a blouse for $25 needed to be a lot more attractive than one costing $14.

When our sons were little, they seemed to have an insatiable appetite for stickers and other small doodads found at the checkout counter. To cope with the situation, we created an allowance book to help them learn to budget at ages three and five. The guys quickly learned that when dollars were spent, the log book might show zero, creating a problem when they later found something really desirable. Similarly, going into temporary debt for a prized purchase meant that less was available, later.

At any age, budgeting controls the inflow of stuff. Here it's good to make a list in advance of going shopping. And stick to it, being careful of buying things on impulse. In the case of major purchases, it helps, also, to jot down the price range next to the item.

It's good to develop habits of stuff budgeting before being faced with hardship or emergency. Since the long downturn that began in 2008, the media have been full of reports about people faced with sudden loss of a job or unexpected medical expenses. As we prepare for the long haul, it's better to develop restraint before hard circumstances force us to learn in a hurry and to play catch-up when times are really tough.

Financial acumen is not the focus of the Stuff Cure, but it can be part of controlling the inflow of things. To this end, we may avail ourselves of various resources for money management, including websites, such as Mint *www.mint.com*, financial software, magazines, and courses at your local adult school.

A related approach is termed *unconsumption*, a new word denoting a lessened level of consumership. Unconsumption includes caring for things so that they last longer, finding new uses for objects, and getting rid of worn out or obsolete material in the most responsible way.[3]

There's a saying that "it's possible to have anything, but impossible to have everything." Here again we find support for the idea of making priorities and allocating our resources to support these objectives.

RETURNING

Even when restraining consumption, we still make mistakes. Ever bought something and then, at home, realized that you acted rashly? Under the influence of a friend, Betty once bought a gown that featured a long fish-tail skirt. Mike gently pointed out that the outfit wasn't particularly flattering nor did it complement Betty's existing wardrobe. The dress went back to the store the next day.

What to Return

What to return? We can begin with issues of quality. As part of our wedding-gift registry, we specified a pattern of fine glassware to go with our good dishes. It soon became apparent that the manufacturer's quality control left much to be desired. As the glasses arrived from different gift shops and stores, we were amazed that they were of noticeably different heights when placed side by side. We decided to do without formal stemware and went for cash. We eventually found some family-heritage used glasses that work just fine.

Of course, returning a gift raises the question of the giver's feelings. In the case of our deficient glassware, Betty wrote her thank-you's immediately, and we were later upfront about deciding to do without formal stemware. Forthrightness combined with tact probably will satisfy most gift givers.

Sometimes the issue is not one of quality but one of appropriateness. On a trip to Edinburgh, Scotland, Betty was torn between two lovely amber pendants, one of art deco style, and the other of much more traditional design. Practical as ever, Betty sprang for the more conventional item. But all through lunch, Betty kept thinking and thinking about her purchase. It became increasingly clear that the art deco piece would be a truly unique and flattering addition to her jewelry box.

So she exchanged the plainer one for the fancier, and she still wears that art deco amber, often receiving compliments for its very unusual pattern.

When to Return

Although most stores permit returns within a few days of purchase, a same-day or next-day policy is probably the best. In fairness both to yourself and to the store, it's prudent to return the item while memories are fresh. Furthermore, if you wait too long, the item is subject to damage and the receipt may disappear.

When you must make a return, remember that you are imposing a bit on the goodwill of the merchant. It's not the seller's fault that you have changed your mind about a purchase or are ambivalent about a gift. On the other hand, stores are looking to build a roster of loyal customers. So if you are careful—keeping the goods in good shape—and are reasonable in relation to store policy, it's likely that things will work out well for all concerned.

REUSING

When Betty and Mike were planning their wedding, Betty enjoyed trying on wedding dresses in the local shops. After the novelty had worn off a bit, Betty began to realize that her top choices were of a style exactly like that of the dress her sister-in-law, Judy, had worn the previous year. Eventually, both Betty and Judy were very happy to see the dress serving as the centerpiece of a second wedding.

> ### THE 7 MORPHS— A FULL CURE:
> **Refraining**
> **Restraining**
> **Returning**
> **Reusing**
> **Renting**
> **Recycling**
> **Rendering into trash**

Re-use is not limited to just the big-ticket items. It's possible to make a daily habit of getting extra value out very ordinary things. Worn out dishtowels may have a second life as rags. Paper towels can be rinsed out, dried, and used again for spot cleaning. Paper grocery bags are very amenable for packaging otherwise miscellaneous recycled paper. Mike's mother even washed her lightly used aluminum foil for later purposes.

Adaptive Reuse: Clothing

As the case of Betty's wedding dress shows, clothing is a particularly apt category for adaptive reuse. In many families, children's hand-me-downs are a time-honored reallocation of clothing. In addition, "hand-me-ups" represent such cases as when a boy, now bigger than his mom, has outgrown a flannel shirt or a sweatshirt that mom can appropriate. Here we should remember that it doesn't improve relationships or family harmony to force clothing on an unwilling recipient. Except in the case of very small children, clothing seen as a castoff may damage feelings of self worth. In such a case, better to donate or redeploy as rags.

Note that it's even possible to adaptively reformat clothing into something new. Maria's mother was very talented as a seamstress and made for her daughter a beautiful, multicolored knit dress. Mom later reformatted the garment as a sweater vest in Maria's adult size.

Looking for a Two-Fer

Sometimes we can unstuff and at the same time solve another problem. For instance, we used to be annoyed by the typical lack of hangers in hotel closets. Our solution? We collect the wire hangers leftover from Mike's all-cotton shirts returned from the laundry. We pack 10 or so in our suitcases, and after using them, we leave these laundry freebies in the hotel room when checking out. This very practical solution also has the side benefit of keeping pointy wires out of the garbage where they pierce plastic trash bags.

Cooperative Reusing

In a similar instance of multiple usage, groups of neighbors sometimes cooperate to share garden and household tools. Passing around garden tillers and other such communal equipment actually was more common in the mid-20th century. Not only were incomes and garages smaller, but in the Eisenhower era—before air conditioning and multiple family cars—neighbors spent more time interacting with one another. But with people economizing more and more these days, the motive of cooperative buying seems ever more opportune for items only occasionally used.

Take the case of six families in Illinois who bought a $1,200 wood chipper such that each could turn branches into wood chips for gardening. In the spirit of "many hands make light work," these neighbors undertook the work cooperatively and then shared the resulting mulch. In addition to the cost savings, everyone enjoyed building a spirit of community.[4]

We can also learn from four families in Connecticut that decided to share a pair of pet hamsters. Each family kept the friendly rodents for six weeks and then passed the pair off to the next household on the list. The benefits were many—and were not limited to cost savings. The children found that they enjoyed having a little time off from their duties of caring for the pets. Families also were able to plan trips without worrying about how the hamsters would be cared for.[5]

In the case of both the wood chipper and the hamsters, one family took the lead in organizing the neighbors. All it really took was one innovative person to get the ball rolling.

Reuse and Creativity

Our kids' kindergarten teacher, Mrs. Randolph, was a pro at adaptive and creative reuse. She delighted the children by helping them turn old salt boxes into castles or towers. In preparation, Mrs. Randolph would send home a list of items for families to save, and the kids would contribute these castoffs to projects. We admired not only her creativity in teaching children to apply their imaginations but also her collateral thriftiness and stewardship of the planet.

Reuse is fundamental to the economy as when scrap gold and silver are melted down or when diamonds are refashioned in new jewelry. Artists and crafters have particularly keen eyes for creative reuse possibilities. We have seen jewelry made out of champagne bottle tops, note cards composed of wine labels, and cheese trays fashioned from flattened bottles. The appropriately named "Reusable Usables Creative Arts Center" in LeClaire, Iowa sells people's discards as raw materials for creative projects by others. The store accepts donations and publishes a wish list based on what their customers are seeking.[6]

As the case of Mrs. Randolph shows, the principle of reuse is available to individuals in everyday situations. If you have unused towels and blankets, you can donate them for reuse at a local pet shelter or veterinary clinic. You might also move along your old linen by checking Annie's Blankets *www.anniesblankets. org* for a list of local donation stations. For other objects you might start with

Earth 911 *www.Earth911.com*, a web address that provides a directory of local reuse and recycling options. For example, your old, but still serviceable, yoga mat may be redistributed to another person at Recycle Your Mat *www.recycleyourmat.com;* you may also use this web address for recycling old and unusable mats.

With some creative thought, people can almost always find a reuse alternative that is superior to putting something in the trash. Consider the case of a husband who, as described in a *New York Times* letter written by his wife, liked to find and repair old umbrellas. When it rained, this good-Samaritan-hobbyist would tote along some of his repaired umbrellas, distributing them to needy pedestrians. His good deeds always brought smiles of gratitude.[7]

Limits of Reuse

Reuse can be overdone, of course. Consider the case of Betty's Aunt Daisy, whose extreme sense of thrift extended to tissues. She called this initiative "half a Kleenex for half a sneeze." Daisy's practice was to tear a tissue in half, and only use one of the two parts. Needless to say, this idea didn't ever catch on among other members of her household.

Betty never bought into Daisy's extreme thrift; but some of this spirit must have rubbed off given certain economies that Betty practiced in her early working years. Needing to dress professionally from a young age, Betty had a large stock of panty hose. When one leg of the hose suffered a snag, Betty would cut off the ruined leg but hang on to the pants plus the remaining good leg. "Johnny one-legs" was her term for these one-legged panties. Betty could then put together two of these half-complete hose and save a bit of money. But the double pants meant that comfort would be a casualty. Furthermore, this degree of discomfort supplied a constant reminder of cheapness. A better solution would have been to select some alternate clothes and a look that avoided the need to wear panty hose every day. For example, we now see young professional women wearing slacks with socks or wearing sandals.

All this is to say that reuse can be overdone when applied to products that are essentially disposable. Yet even disposables have their appropriate reuses as, for example, when old hose are repurposed as filters for clothes dryers lacking an outside vent.

RENTING

It's not necessary to own if you can rent. Renting has become so common that Trendwatching, an Amsterdam-based market–research firm, has coined the term "transumer." According to Reiner Evers of Trendwatching, transumers live a lifestyle that is "less about treasure and more about pleasure."[8]

You've probably never thought of your library card as a rental contract; but the principle is the same. Your taxes are your fee, and you only pay additional charges if you are late in returning books. Your metropolitan library rental arrangement also includes lots of other things: using a computer for free, accessing the Internet, reading current magazines, and your child's playing with puzzles.

If you look around, you'll find many other occasions for renting rather than owning. How about a Christmas tree? Some folks turn to a plant-service firm that delivers and sets up the tree, still living in its pot. The service afterwards picks up the tree, replanting it for the next year's holidays. Don't like to cut grass? Our friend, Ryan, regularly rents a herd of five goats and one llama as a way of trimming his steeply sloped field. When the wild grass and weeds are cleared, the animals move on to their next assignment.

When to Rent

Renting is often the best option for items that (1) you will use only occasionally or (2) you won't need to own on a long-term basis. A rental store in our area advertises with the slogan: "rent the tools, keep the memories."

But it's not necessary to limit renting to chore-related activities. Renting DVDs, as an alternative to buying them, has been popular since the late 1990s through the services of Netflix *www.Netflix.com* and Blockbuster *www.Blockbuster.com*. For those who like to physically sort through the merchandise, brick-and-mortar stores for DVD rentals continue to be a factor; they may be identified by zip code at I Rent 2 U *www.irent2u.com*. Now, of course, you can rent movies entirely in your own home by means of an on-demand, streaming service. Netflix now delivers more movies via download than via the mail.

As evidence of how episodic renting can enhance one's routine, some folks have applied the principle to designer clothes. Such wardrobe enhancers are available at the website Wear Today Gone Tomorrow *http://www.weartodaygonetomorrow.com/*.

This site displays the catchphrase: "who wants to be seen in the same dress twice anyway?" In like manner, you can rent precious jewelry and luxury handbags at Avelle *www.avelle.com*. Rent the Runway *www.renttherunway.com*, offers the motto: "love, wear, return." They even handle the dry cleaning. For those who want to shop locally, retail stores in major cities sometimes reply in the affirmative to inquiries about renting apparel. After all, men have rented tuxedos and formal attire for years for special occasions. In Japan, women rent their bridal attire as the customary practice. Renting formal clothes for special occasions makes especially good sense.

Less Risk If Renting

Avoiding upfront costs is probably the major motivation for renting. When we were first married, we bought a small house. Our budget didn't allow buying all the furniture we might have liked initially. We bought our bed and a dining table while our living room sat empty. When we had overnight company, we would rent a bed and put it in the living room as a guest room. Our parents, our only overnight guests, supported our desire to live within our means and celebrated with us that our moving load was light when we moved out of that house.

Apart from costs, renting also minimizes the risk of obsolescence that always comes with ownership. This principle applies well to tuxedos—and so most people are familiar with renting them. In the case of our own 1973 nuptials, our sons laugh whenever they look at wedding pictures showing the men outfitted in very wide labels and bell bottom trousers—all complete with a polyester sheen. Thank goodness we rented those tuxes.

Peer-to-Peer Renting

A new type of renting, called peer-to-peer renting, has emerged with the assistance of the Internet. Sites such as Zilok *www.zilok.com*, Rentalic *www.rentalic.com*, Snap Goods *www.snapgoods.com*, and Craig's List *www.craigslist.com* enable people to post descriptions and prices of personal belongings that are available for rent. Such rentals might include a guest room in your home, that might be attractive in connection with a local event, or a recreational vehicle suitable for a weeklong trip. Cooperative rental sites have emerged since the recession of 2008 as people seek creative ways to maximize income.

Peer-to peer renting is part of a larger phenomenon that authors Rachel Potsman and Roo Rogers have termed collaborative consumption. In their book, *What's Mine is Yours*, they expand upon the larger idea of how people may have access to things without owning them. We may expect this trend to increase in popularity. Popular not only for reasons of economy but also in view of today's increasing sense that the shared reusing of things helps minimize our environmental footprint as well as giving us more connection to our communities.

RECYCLING

During the last decade, Americans have become increasingly familiar with recycling as local governments implement policies to reduce the volume of trash heading for the dump. Our own home county of Monterey, California, reflects this trend. The Waste Management service charges progressively larger fees for trash containers of increasing size; in contrast, the bin for recycling costs nothing. The shift to recycling has had a tangible impact in lessening waste. In 1990, the local landfill was predicted to have enough capacity to last only until the year 2030. The landfill site now is expected to have capacity through 2140.[9] Many small efforts, indeed, can add up to some big impacts for the environment.

Information about recycling is becoming increasingly accessible. Most communities have a website that discusses recycling policies and opportunities specific to your location. Plastic items typically are marked with a recycling symbol further to help you decide how best to interface with your local waste management policies. Nevertheless, we have found that two categories of items pose particular challenges for recycling. Paper recycling can be difficult because of the large volume of printed materials coming into our homes. Electronic trash— e-waste—can be tricky because of rules relating to hazardous materials.

Paper Control

The clutter associated with paper mounts up as a result of newspapers, magazines, financial reports, catalogs, flyers—to say nothing of cardboard packaging and paper associated with family members' various professional and school projects and hobbies. Both the weight and the volume of castoff paper can be considerable. Yet much of this material is suited for recycling.

The particular problem of paper is that it tends to pile up if you don't have a way to keep it managed. To deal with the influx, we have earmarked a physical location in our home that we call "Paper Control." This space is located in one of our cabinets behind some closed doors. Here we have separate spots for unread mail, unread/half-read newspapers and periodicals, and paper ready for recycling. We use grocery bags to collect whatever paper has been earmarked for recycling—including relatively small paper boxes. Just before the recycling truck arrives, we transfer the bag of recycling to our recycling collection bin—earlier whenever we have accumulated multiple bags.

Most of what goes into weekly paper recycling is the daily newspaper. However, even if you've taken to reading the news entirely online, you will still find plenty of papers piling up if you take into account boxes of consumables such as for cereal or Kleenex. Even when flattened, paper boxes take up a lot of space in the trash can and also come with corners that are perfect for ripping plastic trash sacks. Here it helps to take apart small boxes at their glued edges and then tear along the folds. The flattened paper easily slips into the recycle bag.

In addition to putting out recycle paper on a weekly basis, we periodically sort through the other categories in the Paper Control area. Whenever the space allotted for U.S. mail or periodicals fills up, we go through and cull out what has become obsolete. We've also developed a practice of marking magazines and catalogs on an ongoing basis to indicate that they have been read and used.

This ongoing combing of what comes in the mail represented a change for us. We used to save unread periodicals and catalogs in hopes that we would fully read them someday when we had more time. Instead, we now either recycle this material promptly or, occasionally, save certain magazines to share with friends. It's also possible to drop off magazines and the like at sites such as a Senior Center.

Here we should note that certain financial paperwork needs to be shredded before disposal. Anything that displays your name or account number falls into this category. It's easy to purchase a home shredder to handle the task. You can also take your paper to a shredding and disposal service, such as that offered by Office Max *http://www.officemax.com/catalog/category.jsp?catId=cat1860780*. Shredded paper can be a bit bulkier than flattened sheets; but it is still possible to package shredded material for paper recycling.

E-Waste and Specialized Recycling

The average household in the U.S. now has 25 electronic devices. This adds up, nationally, to over three billion electronic products, with a turnover rate of 400 million products each year. Less than 14 percent of these gadgets are currently being recycled.[10]

You might want to begin with checking whether your castoff electronics are saleable. It may be possible to sell your devices at Gazelle *www.gazelle.com* where they reuse or recycle items. The U.S. Environmental Protection Agency *http://www.epa.gov/wastes/conserve/materials/ecycling/* has a site which answers questions about how to recycle electronic gear. This site also provides locations by zip code where you can donate or drop off used equipment. A related site is e-Stewards *www.e-stewards.org* which gives advice relating to the proper disposal of e-waste. Electronics Take Back Coalition *http://www.electronicstakeback.com* also has information about how to recycle e-waste. If you have put all your music on your iPod or phone, you can recycle CDs, DVDs, and videotapes at Green Disk *www.greendisk.com* or Recycle Washington Eco Disk *www.ecodisk.com*. To locate e-waste recyclers in your area, check out My Green Electronics *www.MyGreenElectronics.org*. For all types of recycling, Earth 911 *www.earth911.com* helps you locate a recycling center near your home for each different type of material.

As you gain experience with recycling, and become more familiar with local and national policies, you'll probably find that the weekly volume of your recycling exceeds that of your trash. Think through your routines so that every member of the family knows how to participate in the recycling effort. Once recycling becomes a household habit, everyone will feel good about reducing the amount of useable and reusable materials that, otherwise, would be wasted in landfills.

RENDERING INTO TRASH

Trash occurs as a normal and necessary part of our lives and can never be completely eliminated. As part of the Green Garbage Project, Amy and Adam Korst tried to live for a year without generating any trash; and the sum total of the couple's trash for 12 months amounted to four pounds. See Green Garbage Project *http://greengarbageproject.adammathiasdesign.com/*. Amy's and Adam's trash included eight used razor blades, a burned-out light bulb, two Theraflu pouches, and a broken Christmas tree ornament.

In contrast to the Korsts, the average American generates four pounds of trash every day rather than over the course of a year. Naturally, the Korsts had to change some of their behaviors to achieve their goal of throwing away less. But the process of change turned out to be so comfortable that Amy later commented: "There's no way I could go back because it ended up being so easy."[11]

Yet trash remains unavoidable in some cases. Things consumed, broken or worn may be unrepairable or unsuitable for recycling. So it may help to take a closer look at the definition of trash.

What is Trash?

The U.S. Environmental Protection Agency defines Municipal Solid Waste (MSW)—popularly called "trash" or "garbage"—as consisting of product packaging, newspapers, clothing, bottles and cans, food scraps, grass clippings, furniture, appliances, consumer electronics, and batteries. The EPA reports that, in the U.S., the quantity of MSW annually generated grew steadily from 88 million tons in 1960 to over 251 million tons in 2006, an increase of 185 percent. On a per capita basis, Municipal Solid Waste generation increased from 2.7 pounds per person per day in 1960 to 4.6 pounds per person per day in 2006.[12]

Specialized Trash Removing Services

For ordinary disposal, the household trash receptacle normally suffices for things that cannot be reused, repurchased, or recycled. In some cases, such as for porcelain toilets and old television sets, families require some kind of specialized trash removing services, either from the regular municipal trash service or from a specialized organization. In both cases, there's likely to be an extra disposal fee. Naturally, costs go up the more you have to get rid of. Looking on the bright side, however, as we encounter problems disposing of trash, we are reminded to be more reticent about future shopping.

If you are burdened with exceptionally large quantities of trash needing to be removed, there are specialized services that will take it away for you. Two of these are: 1-800-Got-Junk *http://www.1800gotjunk.com/* and College Hunks Hauling Junk *http://www.collegehunkshaulingjunk.com*. One such local firm in our own community promotes the motto: "Hauling Is My Calling—Garage and Total House Cleanouts." Trash-removing services sometimes include recycling as part of their business model and profit stream, so some of your trash may have a second life as recycling.

A managed, do-it-yourself approach to extra-volume trash is available from a national service called Bagster *www.thebagster.com*. You buy the Bagster bag for about $30.00 at such home-improvement retailers as Home Depot, Lowes, or Ace Hardware. You then fill the bag and schedule a pick-up with Bagster either by phone or online. The fee for pick-up typically will be in the range of $50-$100. Before committing yourself, you'll want to carefully read the instructions for what types of trash can be included in the Bagster.

Hi Ho, Hi Ho (It's Off to Work We Go)! Throughout this chapter, we've mentioned the payoffs—varying from cash to environmental citizenship—that come with systematically controlling clutter. Our guideposts have been the seven morphs:

refraining
restraining
returning
reusing
renting
recycling
and
rendering into trash

Here we say again that the system is not difficult—and can be fun! Remember that Snow White's seven dwarfs actually sing a catchy tune as they set off each morning to dig for diamonds and rubies in their mine—Hi Ho, Hi Ho (It's Off to Work We Go)! Don't be surprised if you find yourself equally happy about the savings and satisfactions that come from living a life freed from excess accumulation and disorganized clutter.

To help you further incorporate Stuff-Cure changes into your daily routine, we've laid out a framework that we call the Stuff Cure Method. This set of steps, presented in Chapter 6, will help you customize your own process for living a better organized life, one less burdened with unused and unusable things.

• thestuffcure •

6

PLANNING FOR PROGRESS: THE STUFF CURE METHOD

After sixth grade, Betty's family moved from Kent, Ohio to Columbus, Ohio. Betty packed a number of precious keepsakes in one particular 12 x 18-inch box. With the excitement of starting seventh grade in a new town, the years passed without Betty ever digging into that special box.

Fast forward 17 years. Betty and Mike, now married, have returned from Texas to the Midwest, giving Betty's father his first opportunity to unload some of Betty's old things long stored in Columbus. Betty's father happily included the box—labeled "Betty's Kent Stuff"—in a carload of treasures brought to our new home. But Betty and Mike were always too busy to attend to that box. "Betty's Kent Stuff" remained unopened after four family moves—two of them cross-country. Years later, with two boys in college, Betty and Mike finally got around to that well-traveled cardboard cube sealed up for over a generation.

Excavating the old box from Kent was somewhat akin to unearthing a time capsule. Rightly do you wonder what incredibly valuable treasures emerged from this archaeological dig. The inventory included the following: some well-loved girl toys, which really didn't meet modern safety standards; a fake pearl attached by a safety pin to a piece of velvet—something that Betty thought was very pretty when she was six years old; and awards from Betty's days as a Campfire Girl. Betty and Mike took stock of everything, repacked useable things to donate or recycle, and put the rest in the trash.

Initially chagrined at having hauled around and stored useless trinkets for four decades, we eventually recognized that inventorying this old box did have some positive value. Maybe the things weren't worth keeping; but we had learned some lessons that helped us along the road to formulating the Stuff Cure Method.

Our chief learning was that the uncluttered life requires motivation and action. The Stuff Cure Method, as we show below, is all about (1) motivation, in the form of keeping sight of the benefits, and (2) action, in the form of staying committed to a process consisting of seven basic rules. You will find that The Stuff Cure Method can become your own personal action road map for successfully curing headaches associated with your own hoard of possessions.

FOCUSING ON THE WINS

Keeping an old box long unopened reflects the all-too-human tendency to procrastinate with respect to stuff. While our family saved time and effort by keeping undisturbed some of our old boxes, still we suffered costs relating to mover's charges and lessened space in our storage areas. Why couldn't we see the wins in unstuffing—and get to these wins earlier? Why wasn't unstuffing a priority for us? What might have motivated us earlier?

What we needed was a vision of what a win might be for us in really curing our stuff habit. By focusing on unstuffing as a chore, we missed the possible gains. We overlooked or discounted the real burdens of living amid too many things and too much clutter. We hadn't begun to imagine the joy of daily living in an environment of just the right stuff for the life we wanted.

Eventually we became adept at focusing on positive results. Both large and small, the gains from following the Stuff Cure manifested themselves quickly. So let's take a look at what you may expect as you keep your eye on the prize. You'll find that the wins include: adventure, appearance, convenience, satisfaction, and savings.

Adventure

Opening up our stored stuff can be a fun look-see. With just a little imagination, it is possible to think of working through old boxes as an exciting voyage of discovery. From this vantage point, unstuffing is less like a chore and more like opening a time capsule of our lives. And we need not fear entering a kind of Pandora's Box as long as we keep in mind the three criteria for what to keep— useful, sentimental, and valuable.

Betty and Mike once set up an afternoon of unstuffing for adventure when our boys were home for Thanksgiving. Years before, when we left the family home where the boys had grown up, we packed all their Lego toys in seven medium-sized moving boxes. Inside these boxes were plastic sacks containing different Lego sets in partially-assembled form together with loose pieces and instructions.

Our seven big boxes contained all kinds of Lego sets—Castle Legos, Town Legos, Forrest Legos, Boat Legos, Train Legos, Old-West Legos, Space Legos, Technic Legos, and loose Lego pieces.

Hours of real family fun ensued when the boys sorted through the Lego sets, deciding which ones to keep and which ones to donate. Because our sons were now out of college, one of the rules for sorting was that any Legos kept went with the brother who wanted them. But what a hoot it was to remember holidays past and rainy afternoons of yesteryear when the guys and their friends set up whole cities of Lego buildings, vehicles, and people.

Appearance

Important guidelines for interior design include simplicity, functionality, and beauty. For this reason, unstuffing delivers an important win in appearance. Here we admire the look of our space without clutter—as when we open a drawer and see its entire contents in one glance. The completely empty drawer represents a metaphor of our life; it reminds us that we are open to receiving new stuff and new ideas.

The aesthetics of the Stuff Cure don't just apply to drawers and closets: entire rooms and whole houses just look better when uncluttered. Spacious, minimal rooms look luxurious. Crowded Victorian parlors notwithstanding, the 21st century is all about functional and elegant simplicity.

Creating a neat appearance in our home can even be a gift we give to those with whom we share our home. Emma's husband, Benjamin, gave the gift of an unstuffed garage to his wife for her birthday. Because a lot of the clutter in their garage was "his junk," Ben sculpted a neat garage as a special present that surprised his wife when she came home after work.

Moving from the garage to the inside of our residence, we find that an uncluttered house becomes a metaphor for hospitality—it creates a feeling that we are able to welcome guests at any time. From our years in West Texas, we have retained a show-the-house custom from that very hospitable part of the country. Folks there often take visitors through the entire home when their friends come by for the first time.

After adopting the Stuff Cure, we don't panic when family or friends come over for an unexpected visit. We feel confident as hosts because our house looks orderly and uncluttered on an ongoing basis. We don't have to restrict their visit to the front room, because the entire house stays presentable all the time. In these days of residential downsizing, people do not require a McMansion to feel pride in where they live. However modest, a home looks beautiful when it attractively arranges a minimum of functional things without clutter. Our own residence even feels larger without the piles of stuff sitting around and with closets cleared of unnecessary gear.

Convenience

You probably can think of several wins in household convenience that might get you started unstuffing. How about cleaning out a drawer for starts? Try imagining opening up your closet and seeing only clothes that fit. Would making room in the garage for that new car represent an important convenience?

Convenience-oriented wins pay off on a daily basis. Finding that your clothes are ready to wear will save you precious moments whenever you dress. Walking through the basement storage area without having to turn sideways is a plus in locating something stored. The same applies to opening a closet door without having to repack what falls out. Day-to-day living goes more smoothly absent these little frustrations.

Uncluttered convenience can be financially valuable. Real estate agents staging a property affirm this truth every time they advise sellers to clean out their rooms before listing. Take a cue from professional home-stagers who use only the minimum furniture and accessories to suggest the function of each room. Such a sparse environment permits prospective buyers to see themselves at home.

The value of the space gained in our home can be quantified. Begin by estimating the number of square feet you have freed up; multiply this figure by the going rate per square foot in your area. You may also measure your achievement by the bills you have avoided for renting a storage locker.

In assessing the benefits of unstuffing, don't forget the family automobiles. To look at America's garages, a visitor from outer space would never guess that their original function was to protect cars from the elements. On the one hand, your car becomes more conveniently accessible from a dry garage than from a street variously damp, snowbound, windy, or blisteringly hot. Furthermore, keeping the garage ready for the car every night extends the vehicle's good appearance and longevity.

Satisfaction

Measurement is also applicable to satisfaction. Applying the philosophy of Weight Watchers to the Stuff Cure, it's helpful to undertake periodic weigh-ins to assess progress. In both situations, seeing incremental reductions motivates people to continue—and to feel good about their efforts. Because unstuffing takes time and effort, it helps to keep sight of actual progress toward goals; interim milestones demonstrate our successes.

Identifying progress towards goals helps us manage the emotions associated with unstuffing. Instead of mourning the loss of toys from our childhood, we can reflect upon the two cubic feet gained and the $18.00 saved in future moving expenses. In addition, there's the intangible but important satisfaction of knowing we have completed chores postponed for years. Expanding our vision a bit, we may also take satisfaction in doing our part to help sustain the Earth's resources by moving things along to better uses and places.

Savings

As suggested to this point, an Unstuffed Life ultimately improves the cash flow. The key objectives of gift, shift, and thrift are all about saving money by getting greater utility not only from our things and home but also from avoiding storage costs. Sales, tax savings, and consuming less all act to reduce our outflow of cash.

Balancing income and consumption is desirable in general; but outside events sometimes magnify the benefits. The Great Recession that began in 2008 has taught Americans a lasting lesson that it is both possible and prudent to live with less. As the economy has recovered, some will return to old habits of spending that produced overstuffed closets, garages, and attics—and that produced the storage industry. Others will continue to embrace principles of the Stuff Cure to live with less in the present and, correspondingly, to save more for the future.

As you implement principles and tools of the Stuff Cure, you will find it helpful to reflect back on the five key motivators that we have categorized: (1) adventure, (2) appearance, (3) convenience, (4) satisfaction, and (5) savings. With eyes focused on one or more of these prizes, we are better able to stay motivated.

At this point, it's useful to invoke the idea of unstuffing as akin to winning a game well played. As we execute Stuff-Cure plays according to the rules, we may visualize ourselves standing on a winner's platform and showing off our gold, silver or bronze medals for Unstuffing. Let the games begin!

KEEP FOCUS ON THE WINS:

Adventure

Appearance

Convenience

Satisfaction

Savings

RULES OF THE GAME

Motivation gets us started; but only sustained action delivers results. The metaphor of "Rules of the Game" suggests that there are certain ways to optimize unstuffing. This most productive path consists of rules—often low-key hints—that help us map the route of least resistance along that path toward an Unstuffed Life.

The game analogy is additionally appropriate because we who aspire to follow the Stuff Cure are trying to score points against a powerful opposition team. Our opponents field a starting lineup consisting of chore-focused thinking, natural human procrastination, the tendency to blame others for the mess, and the fear that getting organized will open a Pandora's Box of conflicts about whose stuff should be where.

We're up against a powerful opponent, yes. But as the Psalmist reminds us, "fret not thyself."[1] Following the advice of Psalms, we first look to our higher motives—such as our God-given attraction to cleanliness, hospitality, family solidarity, and making a better world. We then rely confidently upon a set of seven common-sense action rules that are laid out, below.

These, then, are the rules of the Stuff-Cure game:

> Rule 1. Seize the moment.
> Rule 2. Look for easy targets.
> Rule 3. Develop a plan.
> Rule 4. Find a staging area.
> Rule 5. Take small steps and repeat.
> Rule 6. Work as a team.
> Rule 7. Don't flip out!

RULE 1. SEIZE THE MOMENT

We begin with seizing the moment, because key life transitions often supply contexts inviting specific action.

At the time of our oldest son's departure for college, we learned that one of our friends, Jill, would need long-term specialized treatment in an out-of-state hospital. Jill's son, Derek, was one of our younger son's best friends; so we suggested to his parents that Derek might stay in our now-vacant bedroom and continue high school uninterrupted.

Needing to prepare an already-stuffed bedroom for a long-term guest, we were spurred to work with John, our soon-to-depart son, to ready his room for a new occupant. We worked to identify what John would need for college, what could be stored, and what might be donated or eliminated. We were all amazed at how much space could be found in a room that, otherwise, would have remained a museum of John's high-school life.

Kids Leaving Home

Although children routinely move out of the parental home—for college, military service, job, marriage—it's easy to slough off this opportunity for unstuffing. In our own case, son John's opening his boyhood room to Derek jumpstarted our family's process of post-high-school slimming down. Even where such a double motivation is lacking, the empty-nest situation represents a transition tailor made for the Stuff Cure.

It's a good life lesson for younger people to imagine their family maximizing the home in their absence. Nevertheless, it's important for the household to treat childhood stuff with some sensitivity. Cases of Mom throwing out the later-valuable comic books are legendary. So it's important that everybody buy into the Stuff Cure as applied to a child's bedroom.

It may be difficult to start unstuffing high-school memorabilia—even though that sophomore-year sweatshirt will soon become totally unfashionable for a college man or woman. So it might be possible to begin with that stack of grade-school art work in the back of the closet—some to save, but much that might become paper recycling. Some of the earliest soccer-team trophies from kindergarten and the early grades probably could be boxed up and moved to less prime real estate. Later, perhaps just one of the trophies could be retained as a representative. Here it's important to remember that unstuffing best operates in degrees and stages. Revisit unstuffing during the first winter break, and regularly thereafter. A little time to mellow helps transform things from outrageously sentimental to sentimental to superfluous to somewhat embarrassing.

A Family Move

A whole-family move seemingly presents the perfect opportunity to apply the Stuff Cure in its full glory. Nevertheless, the stress of the transition sometimes makes it difficult to slim down while needing to pack up. There are long lists of things to do, and decisions must be made by the move-date deadline. Nevertheless, everyone recognizes that unstuffing at the time of a move pays off in terms of savings; and the effort can ease the transition to a new home.

It helps to begin with a vision of your future life in the new home. When we left St. Louis for California, we gladly donated our snow blower, our snow shovels, and a collection of winter coats and boots. Here we looked ahead to our envisioned future in a place of temperate coastal weather with occasional rain during a mild winter. Other objects may be left behind because they no longer are functional for career, for recreation, or for decoration.

Be sure to take advantage of available tools and checklists on the web to assist you in thinking through everything involved in a move. For example, Real Simple *http://www.realsimple.com/home-organizing/organizing/moving/moving-checklist-00000000000208/index.html* has such a checklist. Also you might want to consult an "Improve your Move" e-book at Clutter Diet *http://www.clutterdiet. com/xcart/product.php?productid=16159&cat=259&page=1.*

Ongoing Transitions

We're always making transitions—a new job, a new career, a new season, a new school year. Furthermore we experience changes in needs, changes in technology, along with all the comings and goings of family members. Any of these points of intersection can become opportunities for unstuffing and may bring home the notion that whole categories of items have become superfluous.

Take camping. When our sons were in elementary school, they liked to pitch tents with the Boy Scouts. Once they left for college, the camping gear went to donation because we parents didn't anticipate any more outdoor living. The Scout troop was pleased to receive these items to share with new boys.

Our friend, Manny, used to spend much time in his woodworking shop that was complete with power saws, drills, and routers. Later realizing that his reflexes were not as sharp as the tools he was using, he donated his equipment to a local school's woodworking program.

Changes in technology present regular occasions to reassess our stuff with either elimination or replacement in mind. Betty used to update regularly her three oversized Rolodexes which displayed business contacts by means of hand written or typed cards. Those bulky rolls went by the wayside after Betty began keeping her contacts electronically. Similarly, digital and smart-phone cameras, together with scanning technology, provide easy alternatives to piling up boxes of old prints and negatives.

At a Time of Loss

Some transitions are sad ones, such as when a family member dies. Disposing of a deceased relative's possessions can be a real problem for the family. When there is stuff to be disposed of, family members find themselves needing to act quickly in a highly emotional context. In this connection, however, finding a better home for estate items can become a part of the healing process.

Typically families begin by parceling out items specified in a will, noted in a deceased relative's who-gets-what list, or that fall into the category of generally recognized oral commitments. Where such specifications are murky, or in cases of disagreement, families often use a lottery or a process of alternating selection. All of this should be completed before any contracts are drawn up with a firm that conducts estate auctions.

Community Projects

On occasion, outside agencies present us with an opportunity for an unstuffing project. In St. Louis, Operation Brightside is a community project where bulk items will be picked up by the trash collection agency. Anticipating this pick-up day provides everyone in the neighborhood with a motivation for spring house cleaning, in general. In addition, the event represents a chance to get rid of things that would not fit into the normal trash pick up.

Be on the lookout, also, for notices in the paper soliciting donations for specialized sales. For example, our local Discovery Shop organizes an annual sale of jewelry to raise money for the American Cancer Society. Recently, the Shop reported that they had raised over $18,000.

Inspirational Moments

Returning home from a vacation in Mexico, Barbara Roche Fierman suffered an injury and was taken to the emergency room. When she saw the x-rays taken after the accident, she was taken aback when she tallied 18 pieces of jewelry she was wearing at the time. "From that day I realized how stupid that was. What did I need 18 pieces of jewelry for?" Ms. Fierman has reduced her furnishings to the few things she feels she really needs, such as a Timex watch. "What I learned from the crash, and from some of my clients who are owned by their things, is that it is a ridiculous way of life."[2]

Taking heed of such stories in the media and from friends may be just the push we need to move along the excess material in our lives. Watch for January's "Get Organized Month," an annual event that reminds us all to clear out clutter.

RULE 2. LOOK FOR EASY TARGETS

Whatever beckons us to begin the Stuff Cure, it helps to begin with some small tasks—those that can be completed easily and quickly. Seeing real progress helps you build confidence and induces you to keep on track. However, if something such as an across-the-country move is what brings you to the Stuff Cure, then it may be well to skip ahead to Rule #3 that guides you in developing a comprehensive plan. Nevertheless, looking for quick wins is a proven way to begin making the Cure a fun part of your life.

Just a Junk Drawer?

During one of our moves, the packers asked what label they should use for a kitchen drawer full of miscellaneous stuff. After suggesting "kitchen junk drawer," Betty asked: "Does everyone have a junk drawer?" Our packer replied, "Oh, yes, and you're some of the few people that I have ever packed that have only one junk drawer. Most people have at least three."

So if you want a quick start to your journey of unstuffing, you might think of focusing on one of your junk drawers. On our part, we later determined that there were three categories of stuff in our own such drawer. These miscellanies included: (1) frequently used small items like twisty ties, rubber bands, pencils, and scissors; (2) emergency supplies like a flashlight, candle, matches, and transistor radio, and (3) stuff that didn't have a permanent home and just ended up in the drawer by default.

But the real problem with our drawer of the miscellaneous was its being hard to close and impossible to use. Beginning with consumables such as twisty ties, rubber bands, and coupons, we threw away most of this tangled mass. We then consolidated the rest into ziplock bags, one for each category. Next, we moved the emergency items to a separate drawer exclusively dedicated to such items. Infrequently used tools went to the garage workbench.

Finding Other Targets

Even something as simple as cleaning out a single junk drawer can be in important step in the Stuff Cure. The idea is to define an interim goal—such as a sparser space or more organized stuff—and get started. Congratulations, you're on your way to an Unstuffed Life.

Clothes. Clothes often represent an easy target because our need for them varies based on age, geography, season, time of life, weight, and fashion. If you have ten shirts hanging in your closet, identify one shirt that you can get rid of. Try to manage a 10% reduction for any one category of stuff.

Consumer Reports' ShopSmart magazine reports that the average woman in the U. S. owns seven pairs of jeans but only wears four regularly; one in four women own ten or more pairs of jeans.[3] How about targeting one pair of jeans in your closet that you don't wear that often?

Paper Clutter. As we've noted before, paper is always a problem because it's easy to pile up. Periodicals are particularly prone to linger too long because people think that they, or someone else in the family, may later be reading it. Earlier we mentioned the benefits of having family members mark, or sign off on, a magazine or catalog when it has been read. It's also good to have an agreed-upon shelf-life date after which anyone would be free to place paper items in recycling. Two or three months is a good benchmark.

Freebies. We all pick up give-away items such as bank-promotion frisbees, fun-run water bottles, event-related cups, Happy Meal toys, and the like. Somehow it's hard to throw away freebies even when we're not using them. Start by relegating some of this clutter to donation.

The Storage Question. Whenever you ponder putting things into storage, that's exactly the time to consider getting rid of them. True, it would be hard to give up on that frugally collected box of washed-out jelly jars saved for future household uses. If they're piling up in the pantry, maybe it's time to put them into recycling rather than in a storage locker.

RULE 3. DEVELOP A PLAN

Betty's infamous box of childhood trinkets—labeled "Betty's Kent Stuff"—finally got opened as part of our strategic decision to open and assess all of our unpacked boxes. We set as an objective to unpack at least one box per week. We estimated that it would take us, at this pace, about a year to handle our store of about 50 sealed boxes accumulated from previous moves.

The goal that we set for our 50 long-stored boxes suggests that your own plan for unstuffing need not be complex. All it takes is a simple, shared understanding having three characteristics. First, the plan should set out a goal—such as assessing 50 unopened boxes. Second, it should define a timeline—such as one per week. And third, it should set up an action plan that includes everyone who has a stake in the stuff.

Identify the Goal

Many authorities describe a well-stated goal with the acronym "S.M.A.R.T."[4] This acronym embodies these five elements:

> Specific
> Measurable
> Attainable
> Realistic
> Timely

Begin with the specific and measurable. Identify the areas to be worked on— drawer, closet, garage shelves, et cetera. Measurable criteria can include observable gains in space, organized reductions in clutter, better functionality, and satisfaction among all participants. The related items of "attainable," "realistic," and "timely" are all about motivation and process. Here it is better to start small and build up from early successes.

How Specific a Plan?

For those who like to write down their plans so that everyone will get on board, the family refrigerator door might be used to display targets or objectives. Remember that it's important to get all stuff stakeholders involved. When just a few people are involved, or the targets are simple, an informal shared understanding may suffice.

Define the Timeline

For major projects with a final deadline, it's good to define interim targets along the way. Your intermediate deadlines might involve targeted units (drawers, shelves) or measured outputs (recycling or donation). Modest in-between steps help us avoid procrastination and discouragement. For example, suppose that a local charity makes a pick up of used clothing and household goods in your neighborhood on the second Tuesday of every other month. You might endeavor to put out at least one bag or box for every such pickup.

Replacement Budget

Sometimes major Stuff-Cure projects bring tangible results such as might result from reduced tonnage moved across the country or from consignment sales. Here it is possible to consider the money gained or saved as constituting a kind of replacement budget. Planning for such a budget frees us from needing to hold onto broken tools or worn clothing. We can turn to our budget for replacing them. The replacement budget also works against the ever present fear that we will be disposing of something that we would later need.

RULE 4. FIND A STAGING AREA

When we made our plan to unstuff 50 long-ignored moving boxes, we took advantage of some available space in the basement. Over a period of time, Mike consolidated these boxes into a pile; and we used an adjacent table for sorting through them, one by one.

For major or whole-house projects, it helps to create a designated staging area in an underutilized space. The singer, Fergie, and her actor husband, Josh Duhamel, use a spare bedroom in their home as a "Purge Room."[5] Fergie invites her friends into this room to try on clothes and to take home things that fit them. After her friends take their pick, Fergie donates the rest.

Sometimes a staging area can be temporary. As an example, we mentioned earlier how Mike laid out all the Legos in piles on the basement floor one Thanksgiving. Having the basement floor as a temporary staging area enabled us really to see everything for purposes of sorting. Afterwards, the basement floor was cleared and returned to normal use.

In addition to large-scale sorting areas, it's also possible to maintain a number of smaller such places throughout the house. We have a particular shelf in one closet where we put clothes to be donated. In our garage, we keep a box to collect donatable household items such as freebie plastic cups and bottles.

RULE 5. TAKE SMALL STEPS AND REPEAT

As we've already mentioned, the Stuff Cure is something best undertaken on an ongoing basis. The best results seem to come from taking small steps—but keeping at it, day after day.

10% - 30% at a Time

From long experience, we know that it's difficult to part with more than a fraction of our things at any one time. Our rule of thumb is to attempt getting rid of between 10% and 30% on any given pass.

Take the case of the nine silver bowls we received as wedding gifts. In Betty's first review of silver items, she was able to get rid of three duplicates. After two further reviews, she had unstuffed an additional three bowls on the basis of quality and style. The eventual result was two-thirds of the bowls donated—but it took three separate applications of the Stuff Cure. Had Betty attempted to get rid of most of her beautiful silver bowls at one time, she might have given up in exhaustion or frustration.

The 10-to-30% rule fits well with multiples of clothing. Try this with your socks and tee shirts. If you restrict your unstuffing to just the items with worn spots, holes, or frayed collars, you'll probably have no trouble relegating 25% to donation or to the rag pile. Then later you can review your collection for style, fit, or sentiment.

Keep Things Moving

We cannot emphasize too much the importance of making the Stuff Cure part of your daily routine. Whenever you come across something unfunctional, of low value, or unconnected to sentiment, move it to the staging area. Later you can make a decision about it on your own or ask others in the family to speak up for it if they will. Soon you will find enough volume in your staging area to facilitate a next step such as a donation or garage sale.

Being Proactive

Although we've focused on things already stored for awhile, an important part of the Stuff Cure is proactively managing new stuff. Develop the habit of applying the Cure immediately to whatever comes into the home.

Why not begin with an on-the-spot triage of the daily mail? Some fliers and the like can be recycled on the day of arrival. More important mail, such as bills and letters, can be moved promptly to the desk. Similarly, part of making every new purchase functional is to put it in its proper place. And if shopping is intended to displace something—such as a new skillet for an old one—it's good to immediately move the old item to a staging area for donation.

RULE 6. WORK AS A TEAM

We've already introduced the idea of stuff stakeholders. Even when things clearly belong to one individual, it's possible that others see themselves connected. If an item from Mom's jewelry box is frequently borrowed by daughter, then there are at least two stakeholders for this adornment. It's best for family harmony if all stakeholders are involved in a decision to sell, donate, recycle, or trash an item.

When working as part of a stakeholder team, you find yourself able to see stuff through someone else's eyes. The staging area further makes possible the team approach to unstuffing. When someone finds a favorite knickknack placed in the donate box, they have occasion to take continued or new responsibility for the item—or let go of it.

RULE 7. DON'T FLIP OUT!

When two or more people share a home, they often bring different approaches regarding how to manage stuff. It's common to hear one partner describe the other with terms such as "pack rat" or "piler"—or worse—to reflect negative thoughts about how stuff is taken care of. Most of us learned how to care for stuff from our parents. And our parents developed different approaches to stuff based on circumstances relating to income, size of residence, frequency of relocation, sense of style, frugality, and assumptions about the future.

However much we differ in our approach to acquiring, using, and keeping things, we share objectives relating to a pleasant and functional living space. Here it's important not to move too aggressively or too fast. The team spirit—with a commitment to "no surprises"—is a way to avoid flipping out. Be sure that everyone understands the process—goals, roles, stakeholders, staging areas, and the like. A process both serious and cooperative will help draw out what Lincoln termed "the better angels of our nature."

Here you'll notice that the Stuff Cure is set up to avoid nagging. Emphasis is on conducive moments, easy targets, small steps, specific goals, a recognized staging area, and teamwork. The system is flexible enough that, once begun, the process tends to continue without any one person needing to dominate.

With the seven-step Stuff Cure Method now under your belt, you've assimilated enough material to really start making changes in your life. You know why stuff clings (Chapter 2); you know the three criteria for what to keep—function, value, outrageous sentiment (Chapter 3); you've wrapped your mind around the three key motives of gift, shift, and thrift (Chapter 4); you've gotten a handle on the seven morphs of stuff stewardship (Chapter 5). And now Chapter 6 gives you your road map in the form of seven rules of the game.

Try an experiment. Find a mutually agreeable time and place for some family unstuffing. How about sorting through one shelf of books with the aim of moving along at least a handful of volumes? How about looking over that pile of old shoes and boots in the hall closet—with the objective donating at least one pair to Soles4Souls? How about assembling old eyeglasses for collection by the Lions Club?

Not everyone in the family will have occasion to complete *The Stuff Cure* book. So we conclude this chapter with a single page containing a summary of each of the seven rules. This roster can jumpstart some real downsizing. Post the list on your refrigerator door or bulletin board. Pass it around as a discussion starter. The overall point being that NOW is your moment to begin the Stuff Cure. However modest are your beginnings, the key is to stay motivated, to keep active, and to work together as a family team.

the
stuff
cure

RULES OF THE STUFF CURE METHOD

Rule 1 Seize the Moment — NOW

Rule 2 Look for Easy Targets —
Three Rules: Function, Value, Sentiment

Rule 3 Develop a Plan — What by When?

Rule 4 Find a Staging Area — or Even Two

Rule 5 Take Small Steps and Repeat — Every

Bit Helps

Rule 6 Work as a Team — Everybody Counts

Rule 7 Don't Flip Out! — Fun is the Goal

• thestuffcure •

7

LIVING THE CURE – ROOM BY ROOM

The comedian, Gallagher, used to deliver a popular bit that began with his observation, "I see you have a baby!" Immediately, Gallagher would start to dump toys and other baby paraphernalia all over the stage. Gallagher's comedic take on parenthood rings all too true; this is, indeed, what our living room or bedroom looks like after baby has arrived. It reflects the hopeless situation of parents who can't straighten up a room at the same rate that things are being thrown about.

And as we all know, it doesn't require a baby for us to become overwhelmed by clutter. We've all got rooms that represent a variation on the scene portrayed by Gallagher. And within these rooms are closets and drawers that present a similar picture—things randomly pushed, piled, and strewn.

To this point we've focused on stemming the inflow of things and expediting the outflow. Now we want to lay out a view of the Stuff Cure as it applies to organized, clutter-free living on a room-by-room basis. We're talking about a functional approach for keeping the stuff you need accessible wherever you need it. When we are organized, our rooms, or spaces within our rooms, have specific memorable purposes. This kind of organizing work dovetails with all the suggestions given to this point about downsizing the clutter. As you tighten up the functionality of each drawer, closet, and room, you'll find yourself able to do with much less accumulation in each of these spaces.

We'll start with the public areas of the house—kitchen, dining room, living room, entertainment areas. Then we'll consider the treatment of mail, paperwork, and office functions. Next comes the bedrooms and bathrooms. Finally, the storage locations—workshop, attic, basement, and garage. We'll walk through the house room by room, with focus on organized living with just what we need.

Naturally, you'll be considering all of our observations in the context of your own daily routines. We hope that the combination of our insights and your own experience will start you thinking about how to create a home environment that is both efficient and enjoyable. The bottom line of the Stuff Cure is to make sure that your daily environment is a place you love to be.

KITCHEN

Julia Child's kitchen from her Cambridge, Massachusetts home has been preserved in the Smithsonian in Washington, D.C. From this exhibit, it becomes clear that Julia surrounded herself with only the kitchen tools she needed, and in addition, provided a storage place for everything. You can see pictures and hear her comments at the Smithsonian website *http://americanhistory.si.edu/juliachild/*. Julia hung her pots and pans on pegboard for close access while cooking. She traced the outline of each pan so she knew where to return it to its proper hook.

Professional chefs use the French phrase "Mise en place" (put in place) to describe assembling and organizing ingredients necessary to prepare the meal. TV cooking shows illustrate this concept by means of a tray of pre-measured ingredients that the chef assembles on-camera—an enterprise that culminates in a mouth-watering dish. With a bit of practice, home cooks can use this same principle as a guide for organizing frequently used tools, spices, and ingredients.

Pantry

It's common for people to maintain a pantry area for food staples, such as rice, dry pasta, and canned food. These are ingredients stored and organized so that meals may be prepared with the minimum number of grocery-store trips. Pantry contents should be limited to items having a reasonable shelf life. Sometimes expiration dates are given in small print or are imbedded in a code; so it may be a good idea to jot down the date of purchase with a magic marker. If an item is marked "refrigerate after opening," it's wise to keep it out of the pantry. Otherwise you may be in the position of an older couple we once knew that wondered why they had so many episodes of "stomach flu." Might it have been the blue-cheese dressing stored above the stove?—or the butter softened by keeping it at room temperature out of the refrigerator?

Is your pantry organized on the basis of meal preparation? Or are components scattered haphazardly? Review your setup from the standpoint of what family members use and when. Boxes can be organized on the basis of such basic categories as these: breakfast items such as cereals; cooking-related condiments and oils in another place; canned goods elsewhere ready for lunch or dinner.

You'll be most satisfied with home meals if you expend pantry items in a timely fashion. Keep your inventory low enough that you replace essentials frequently. Place items on the shelves so you can see at a glance what you have—and also keep track of expiration dates. If you find it difficult to regularly shelve taller items in the back, you might consider turntables for easier visibility.

Spices

Herbs and spices are formally defined as plant products used in small quantities to enhance the flavor and/or color of food. Like all botanical materials, spices are best when fresh, although whole spices can be kept up to one year. Ground spices, on the other hand, should be expended within six months of having been made granular. All spices lose flavor as they get old, and some of them may even become rancid. If a spice container looks sticky, cloudy, or if it shows dust on the lid, throw it out.

Spices are best located in a dry space away from light and heat. Sometimes you'd never guess this fact given that contractors often place spice racks near the stove top or next to an oven. Organize your spices in alphabetical order to help you find what you need. Although sunlight doesn't help bottled spices, you'll want to be sure that you've placed the pots for growing fresh live herbs to take advantage of the sun's rays. Cultivating parsley, basil, and chives makes for an attractive mini-garden on your kitchen window sill.

Refrigerator and Freezer

Refrigerators are designed—obviously—to keep perishable food fresh. Such a truism seems all-too-often neglected in refrigerators that are packed so tight that no one can see what's been pushed to the rear. Or consider the common situation of refrigerated items being used on a "last in, first out" basis such that things unseen linger unused.

Check out Still Tasty *www.stilltasty* for answers to specific questions you may have about food safety and flavor. The University of Kentucky extension service offers a complete list of how long different foods can be safely stored without losing their nutrients at *http://ces.ca.uky.edu/oldham-files/FN-SSB.085.pdf*. As a rule of thumb, leftover food should be stored in the refrigerator for no more than five days.

You'll also want to increase the consistency of shelf placement for different types of food—dairy items, soft drinks, et cetera. This way, you can easily check both the quantity and freshness of your supply. Here it helps to label leftovers or opened containers with indication of the date. And it's good to make a habit of cleaning out the refrigerator each week before heading to the store. Any such changes in the organization and management of the refrigerator may require a bit of family discussion.

Wine

"I came for the weather and stayed for the wine." This is how our friend, Martha, explains her relocation to California. For many Californians, and for many Americans across the continent, wine forms an essential part of the gourmet experience.

Even if you don't regularly visit wineries to assemble a collection, and even if you haven't yet invested in a special wine storage unit, you still may glean useful tips from available online resources. You'll learn about the correct temperature for wine storage and such other hints as keeping bottles horizontal so that the corks stay moist. Wine management software, developed originally for restaurants and wineries, may be found at Wine Tech *www.winetech.com*, Cellar Tracker *www.cellartracker.com*, Wine Cellar Software *www.winecellarsoftware.com*, Uncork *www.uncork.biz*, Warpa *www.warpa.com,* and Manage Your Cellar *www.manageyourcellar.com*.

If you are not a passionate wine enthusiast, but do like the occasional bottle, buy just enough for your current needs. In effect you would be outsourcing your wine cellar by finding a wine shop with well-labeled shelves and/or a knowledgeable expert.

Recipes

Recipes—especially for baking family favorites—are an essential part of food preparation. They remind us of the ingredients and steps that, together, produce predictable kitchen successes. Unscripted experimentation works best for experts—and for those who have no fear of wasting expensive food or time.

Naturally, recipes and cookbooks should be stored reasonably close to the food preparation area for ease of access. Individual recipes can be organized on file cards, in a scrap book, in your computer, and/or as clippings kept in manila files. Locate new recipes in one place till they become family favorites.

You may find it worth the trouble to create a more permanent format for accessing and sharing favorite recipes. Here it's possible to employ simple word-processing software, possibly supplemented with self-publishing software, to bring together recipes in online or printed formats suitable for sharing. You can also use tools for assembling your own cookbooks and recipes files at Epicurious *www. epicurious.com* or All Recipes *www.allrecipes.com*.

Emergency Supplies

You don't have to follow the Weather Channel, or the latest disaster covered by CNN, to know that floods, mudslides, fires, tornadoes, ice storms, and earthquakes happen all the time. How prepared are you for a power outage lasting five days? You'll be more prepared if you have a designated space for emergency supplies.

Experts recommend that homeowners designate one space, often a drawer in the kitchen, for storing emergency supplies. Find a location near a window so that the contents can be seen when the power goes out. Keep in that drawer a flashlight, a battery-powered radio, duct tape, some candles with holders, and matches. Also keep some work gloves, a pad of paper and a pencil, a first aid kit, any emergency keys, and emergency numbers for the power and gas companies.

Only emergency supplies should be in your designated crisis location so that you can access things easily, even in the dark. It's OK to use supplies from the drawer—like matches—for routine chores, so long as you make sure the emergency supplies are always fully stocked.

It's good to keep on hand three days of food and water for emergencies. It's helpful to date such boxes, bottles, and cans if you are locating some or all of these items somewhere other than your regular pantry. Remember that during times of emergency, family members will find it more comforting to consume foods and drinks that are simple and familiar.

On Day 1 of the emergency, you'll want to utilize food from your refrigerator. Day 2 is the time to begin using food from your freezer. On Day 3, it's best to shift to dry and canned foods from your pantry. Depending on the size of your pantry, many or all of these items may be treated as part of the regular rotation of staples.

If you live in a remote area, or one that has a history of particular natural emergencies (like earthquakes, floods, or tornadoes), you may want to undertake additional and specialized disaster preparation. Local offices of emergency preparedness will be able to alert you to further precautions and emergency supplies.

Family Schedule

Because the kitchen often serves as a central gathering point, it's common to find here various reminders of the family agenda. The kitchen is often where family members come to find school lunch tickets or invitations—or to access a calendar of events posted on bulletin board, refrigerator door, or computer terminal.

A calendar for listing all appointments and commitments serves as a resource for the entire family. Whether paper or electronic, the principle is the same—everyone needs to know how to access and update entries. If your kitchen doesn't include a desk area, the calendar may be better situated at a work space elsewhere in the house. Maintaining a shared space for weekly and monthly events also helps in preparing end-of-the-year retrospectives that might include holiday letters or tax preparation.

DINING ROOM

Formerly an essential of middle-class life, today's dining room may come into play only for holiday and special-occasion meals. Contemporary houses sometimes are designed without a separate or formal room for dining on the assumption that meals will be taken on a kitchen table, nook, or countertop.

With dining rooms now less functional for the original purpose, many are used chiefly as multipurpose spaces. Often the dining table is perfect for homework, special projects, or such hobbies as sewing, quilting, or assembling model aircraft— all of which activities require a large, clear work surface. Dining-room activities will be facilitated by using an adjacent built-in cabinet or a separate sideboard chest for storing appropriate supplies. Because it is likely that the dining-room space will be shared by all family members, it's good to establish rules about putting away supplies at the end of the day or week. It might be good to dedicate a separate storage container for each family member's projects.

Dining-Room Decor

If you have the luxury of using your room just for dining, organize to optimize the culinary experience. Keep plenty of room around the table to facilitate serving the meal and clearing the dishes. One basic rule of thumb is to allow at least 18" of clearance behind each chair.

From a decorating point of view, it is good to arrange wall hangings so that they will be equally attractive when viewed from both standing and seated positions. The height of pictures and wall hangings should be no higher than the eye level of the tallest member of the family. Measure the horizontal midline of the picture frame and then hang at eye level, usually about 58" to 60" above the floor. Pictures that will be viewed primarily from a seated position should be hung even lower.

Dishes and Good Dishes

In the Victorian Era, having beautiful dishes and silverware signified affluence and good taste. Today, we think about table-service items more in terms of functional utility. Nevertheless, everyone appreciates the loveliness of good dishes, and some families still keep an additional set of dishes, beyond their everyday set, for holidays and special occasions. These less-frequently-used dishes and glassware may have been acquired as wedding gifts from friends or they may represent things having sentimental value from an inheritance.

Special or family-heritage dishes are particularly appropriate for kitchen or dining-room decorating. If you are fortunate to have a china cabinet with glass doors, your dishes and glassware will serve as an attractive display even when they are simply stacked up. If, on the other hand, your good dishes are stored in the attic or basement, it repays to keep them well packed and clearly labeled—as would be the case for a move.

Sterling silver is best stored in protective, non-tarnish bags, or in a similar kind of chest. It also helps to keep the bags wrapped in plastic when silverware, or silver dishes and bowls, are not in use.

> "Have nothing in your house that you do not know to be useful, or believe to be beautiful."
>
> *William Morris, British craftsman, designer, and poet, 1834-1895*

Particularly if your household consists only of adults, consider using your good dishes routinely. With care, glassware, dishes, and silver will last a lifetime. And, as mentioned earlier in the book, online replacements may be readily found in the case of any breakage.

LIVING ROOM

Sometimes off limits to pets and children, the living room traditionally was kept in readiness for special occasions or for unexpected guests. Many houses now lack a formal and separate parlor-type space; so for those fortunate enough to have this extra room, it seems better to transform a "Living Room Museum" into a functional room able to help solve clutter problems in the rest of the house. Which of your family activities might be offloaded into the living room? Possibly an office desk—with or without computer; perhaps a refuge for reading; conceivably the go-to place for playing an instrument, video or board games; maybe the big TV?

Enhancing living-room functionality often begins with the basics of decorating. "Good design is about editing," according to professional interior designer Todd Alexander Romano.[1] Designers build the décor by first selecting a unifying element such as a rug or large piece of art. Next, they create a functional and attractive space by selecting major items that complement the unifying element, and by placing these larger components so that the room works for its intended purpose(s). Photographs of rooms designed by professional decorators reflect a clean, uncluttered look.

The parable of "The Three Bears" is useful for implementing elements of room design. Look at your room and its furnishings through the eyes of Goldilocks, classifying everything into one of three categories: Papa Bears, Mama Bears, and Baby Bears. These categories refer to the relative sizes of pieces—large Papa-like furniture, smaller Mama-like furnishings, and decorative Baby-like accent pieces. Papa Bears and Mama Bears are usually classified as currently functional and sometimes really valuable. Baby Bears are often sentimental.

We begin the process with the Papa Bears, that is, large pieces needing to be arranged first, such as large rugs, sofas, big-screen TVs, or armoires. The arrangement of the Papa Bears reflects how the room will be used and the flow for how people will walk and sit in the room. Arrange your Papa Bears to maximize the utility of the room and the feeling of openness.

Mama Bears represent the medium pieces to be placed after the Papa Bears are arranged—for example, large pictures, end tables, computer screens, cushions, and lamps. The Mama Bears give the room personality and interest. Tired Mama Bears can often be replaced or rearranged to give your room a new look with a minimum of additional purchasing. Use additional lamps to illuminate your room and to make it functional for activities.

Baby Bears constitute the accent pieces that express your individuality and taste, such as coffee table books, glass, art work, candles, reading material, and family pictures. Add Baby Bears to your décor only if they make the room look better. Be mindful of Baby Bears that tend to creep into the room and contribute to a cluttered look. You can return your room to an organized look by counting the Baby Bears and keeping the number to less than seven for the entire room. Baby Bears can be changed with the season or holiday to give your room a fresh look year round. Fresh flowers are wonderful Baby Bears that won't overstay their welcome.

FAMILY ROOM

Depending on the size of your home, you may have a separate family room, media room, and/or play room. Increasingly, the home functions as a center for media-related entertainment—this since the time when radio replaced going to the vaudeville hall and television replaced thrice-weekly attendance at the movies.

Entertainment Media

Home entertainment, nowadays, is based on a range of media forms varying from Internet streaming to printed books. The family room might be outfitted variously as a home theater with plush seating, as a library with built-in bookshelves, or as a music center with state-of-the art speakers.

Whatever the case, media consumption in all forms raises two fundamental issues of clutter. First, accessing content involves the organizing of space—whether it be storing CDs or dusting boxes and wires associated with video streaming. Second, there is the issue of obsolescence—because media change over time. Eventually, old devices must be disposed of and, possibly, new furniture and equipment acquired. Further, older systems often overlap with newer ones, sometimes doubling problems of storage and furnishing. Following are some organizational ideas.

TV/DVR. Is your seating area arranged to facilitate comfort and visibility for the number of persons who typically watch together? Considering the number of hours that we sit in front of the set, it may be false economy to retain uncomfortable or cluttered seating.

Whenever you get a new TV, don't miss the opportunity to recycle your old set at the store where you've bought the new one. You'll enjoy the space savings; and the environment will benefit, also, because both the old-style cathode-ray-tube sets and the new flat-screen ones contain materials that shouldn't be added to landfill dumps. We learned this space lesson the hard way. We once had amassed a total of seven TVs by neglecting to dispose of still-functional, but nevertheless unused, sets.

Have trouble finding the remote? Maintain one place where you keep the remote control and return it to that place when you are closing up for the evening. A survey by IKEA, the home-furnishings retailer, found that men spend an average of 80 minutes per week looking for the remote control.[2] Can't place those DVDs? Special DVD cabinets and shelves are widely available; but these discs also fit conveniently in 16-quart clear plastic storage boxes.

Television delivery has changed greatly from those early days of the wooden TV cabinet controlled by a rotary dial having 13 channels. Digital television requires some kind of control unit, and many Americans increasingly rely on recording programs for later viewing by means of a DVR controller supplied by a cable or satellite provider. Such providers also offer a variety of fee-based programs on-demand. Additional external services include, on the one hand, a DVD player or streaming video ordered from Netflix *www.netflix.com*, Hulu *www.hulu.com*, or Amazon Instant Video *http://www.amazon.com/Instant-Video*. In addition, many people find it either cheaper or more convenient to watch TV shows on their desktop, laptop, iPad, or smart phone via such services as Roku or Apple TV. Given this array of options for watching TV shows or TV movies, you'll want to reflect on what best fits your habits and budget.

Video Disks. Because movies or television series increasingly can be streamed on television or computer, it's likely that you'll be buying fewer DVD or Blue Ray disks. Nevertheless many people will want to keep video-disk copies of particular favorite movies that will be watched many times in the future. Even if you rely primarily upon streaming or on-demand services, you may want to hang onto favorite movies in DVD or Blue Ray format. Retaining these discs not only assures easy availability but also enables one to avoid paying for the same content over and over. In addition, disks can be desirable in view of their often including special features.

DVD or Blue Ray disks have proved to be more durable than the preceding technology of the videotape cassette. Where VHS tapes needed to be carefully stored on end—to keep the tape from sagging in the case—careful DVD storage chiefly involves keeping them covered from dust and keeping the DVD rack or box away from heat sources or direct sunlight. If you have a large number of video disks, it helps to have a printed list of your titles which can then be boxed or racked alphabetically, in general, or by genre (mystery, comedy, children's). It's possible to reduce the amount of space occupied by disks by purchasing Dynex brand or other extra-slim clear plastic cases—this, of course, requiring some cash outlay plus the loss of information contained on the original case.

Music. The piano used to be a requisite in the middle-class parlor. Yet by the 1920s, the phonograph was augmenting what previously had been the common practice of family members entertaining one another with instrumental playing. Even with music now downloaded from such sources as Apple's iTunes Store, Americans still listen to favorite CDs at home or in the car. It often proves the case that that the family room retains some of its traditional musical functions because this room may be the site for the family's most powerful speakers.

Physical storage requirements for our music collection have been greatly reduced by digital technology. Today, it's often the case that our music library travels with us—stored on a compact player or smart phone. People are coming to take for granted the ability to access favorite tunes anytime and anywhere.

But music storage can still be an issue in connection with analog formats. If you or others in your family play an instrument, it's likely that you'll have a collection of sheet-music that exceeds the space available in the piano bench or side-table drawer. Sheet-music can be stored in magazine boxes available at office-supply stores. And they are also suitable for clear plastic storage boxes that may be grouped in a closet.

In addition, for a variety of reasons, music connoisseurs sometimes like to retain older musical formats, particularly 33-1/3-RPM LP vinyl albums. Some have a specialty player with a range of playing speeds that even accommodates antique 78-RPM disks. Each of these analog systems requires some form of disk storage. Phonographic records of all kinds are best stored vertically rather than stacked one on top of the other. They should also be separated with some kind of paper jacket. Check a container store or online storage supplier for alternatives.

Books. In the words of Emily Dickinson (1830-1886), "There is no Frigate like a Book to take us Lands away." Dickinson's sentiments capture what has always been the appeal of the book as a vehicle to transport and entertain us. Furthermore, books sometimes possess an appeal akin to that of familiar, old friends. "Of all the stuff I try to get rid of as an organizer, books are the most difficult," says Leslie Josel, owner of the home organizing service, Order Out of Chaos.[3]

Since the Great Recession of 2008, Americans have turned increasingly to the local public libraries for reading material. And it's also possible to keep up a flow of paperback books through 2-for-1 exchanges at selected used bookstores or by means of other trading arrangements with friends. Nevertheless, it's still common for individuals and families to amass a collection of favorite print titles requiring storage.

Books should be arranged to prolong their condition and utility. Paper media are particularly vulnerable to water, humidity, sun, and insects. Ideally, books should be kept in areas of moderate temperature and of low humidity. For book storage, the main floor of a home is superior to the basement, garage, or attic—and inside walls are better than outside walls. In addition, books should be shelved standing up on the bottom edge or laying flat. They should never be situated so that weight is placed on the spine. The very worst possible storage is that which "breaks the spine," that is, permits gravity to pull the pages down away from the binding.

Organize your books in a way that has meaning for you, such as by subject matter or author. If the books are shelved in your living room, you may want to organize them by height and color of their cover to give a coordinated look. If you have a very large number of books, it may repay for you to maintain a computer document listing the titles in alphabetical or topical format.

Activities

In addition to serving as the prime location for media consumption, the living room may be organized to facilitate games, hobbies, crafts, scrapbooks, memorabilia, and photographs.

Games. Before electronic game players became popular, families liked to play board games, from checkers to Monopoly, or card games including bridge or poker. These pastimes, harkening back to a pre-digital era, still hold appeal in view of their providing face-to-face fun. All you need is a usable table, or set-up card table conveniently stored, plus an accessible place for game pieces. It's good, periodically, to review whether the games you have are actually used.

A game's original boxing is useful for helping you keep track of the individual pieces. It's good to practice a rule of putting games away after they are completed—and making sure that every piece is accounted for. Store the boxes so that they stay closed with contents intact.

Electronic games have their own assortment of bits and pieces. We find plastic storage boxes particularly suited to warehousing components because they can be labeled and stacked on shelves. You'll find it easier to secure a proper storage home for the new game if you displace outmoded systems and all their associated parts.

Hobbies and Crafts. Hobbies and crafts gratify our tactile sense—the pleasure of actually holding something. This is why, even in the electronic age, people gravitate to hobbies that involve collecting things—like stickers, stamps, action figures, or model cars.

Crafts represent a related activity involving put-together projects such as knitting, needlepoint, and model airplane building. You will need to have enough functional storage so that every member of the household not only has access to necessary supplies but also is able to put away projects when they're not being worked on. Where cabinets, closets, or drawers are not available, stackable plastic storage boxes are functional, and not unattractive, when placed in a corner or along a wall.

Scrapbooks and Memorabilia. All of us keep things because of their sentimentality; and many of these mementos come in the form of paper diplomas, certificates, and souvenirs. It's good to take the time to gather paper treasures in files, envelopes, boxes, or scrapbooks. This will facilitate your periodically pruning your collection until it consists of just the most important items stored in a way that permits convenient perusal. What's the point of keeping these things if you can't look at them from time to time?

In our digital age, it's now possible to scan paper materials electronically not only to make them easily available but also to back them up by digital filing. Digital materials—for instance, those related to family genealogy—also are suitable for sharing with family and friends. Digital storage also facilitates making calendars and collages that highlight family photos and memorabilia. Anniversary tributes can be made with historic pictures and souvenirs in scrapbook or video format. It's also possible to reformat digital materials in printed, bound form.

If you want to document the story associated with some of your things, you may want to use Tales of Things *www.talesofthings.com* or Itizen *www.itizen.com.* These services allow you to write or record the story of an item and upload it to the web. You then attach a bar code to the item. Anyone can scan the bar code and be able to access the story associated with the item. You can use this tool for items you want to keep and/or items you wish to sell.

Photos. During the last 20 years, photography has transitioned from film-based methods to digital formats. Yet if you're over 25 years of age, it's likely that you are in possession of a number of paper-print photographs.

Probably you will want to scan some of your favorite paper prints to the web or to disk. However, remember that print-based photographic formats retain value by remaining independent of changes in digital technology. When stored carefully in a dry, dust-free environment, paper photographs can last up to one hundred years. Because paper photos can be scanned, most experts believe that we may dispense with the film negatives. Where your photographs come into contact with folders, files, or paper boxes, it is best that this paper be of an acid-free kind. Ideally, your storage materials would be specifically designed for keeping paper photographs well preserved.

Of course, it's no wonder that digital photography has become so popular. For starts, we save the cost of film and developing—and the need to eat the cost of our photographic mistakes. In addition, digital media permit us to organize images for emailing to friends, for posting online, and even for printing photos in whatever form desired.

Although digital images consume less physical storage space than prints, they still require organization so that we can access them. Here it's likely that we'll want to lay our digital hands on just the right photos to document visually a graduation, wedding, or other special occasion. Most people organize their photos by the date the photo was taken. You can add keywords or tags such as the names of the people in the picture, the location, and the occasion to facilitate searching through your photo database.

A number of websites permit you to capitalize on the wide-circulation capacity of digital photography. You can use social-networking sites such as Facebook *www. facebook.com*, My Space *www.myspace.com*, or Baby Community *www.babycommunity. com* to share pictures. Sites such as Flickr *www.flickr.com* and Picasa *http://picasa. google.com* allow you to share and store photos; and YouTube *www.youtube.com* has become famous as a resource for posting videos. In addition, you may want to access a website that offers you the ability to store, print, and customize a photo book made up of your own pictures. Check out Snapfish *www.snapfish.com* and Shutterfly *www.shutterfly.com*.

OFFICE—PAPER INFLOW AND RECORDS STORAGE

Home is not only where the heart lies but also is the site for transacting business, both personal and financial. The result is a nearly constant inflow of paper, even in this electronic age. Few households are able to dedicate an entire room to home-office functions. Nevertheless, everyone can benefit from maintaining a well-organized space for bill-paying, tax preparation, and managing personal paperwork.

Mail and Paper Control

We've already discussed paper control as part of recycling. But it's useful, here, to expand a bit on how paper figures in household management. It all starts with the mail. With bills, renewal offers, and contribution requests arriving every day, there's always some need for interim storage because it's difficult to process all of our mail on the spot. We used to take the daily deluge out of the mailbox and drop it on a family-room table. Paper would stay piled until the stack grew so tall that it would topple over, demanding attention. As an initial coping strategy, we transitioned to piling the mail on a closet shelf so we could close the door on the problem.

Eventually we learned that simply increasing the size of the piling area was not sufficient for handling mail. What is necessary is an ongoing process for working through what the postman brings. Start with a designated triage area, maybe near your mailbox, but even better near your desk. Sort and classify each piece as you identify it. Place junk mail in a recycling container, immediately, and make sure that important envelopes and papers quickly find a way to a file, a drawer, or tray that contains Action Items. If your household contains many mail recipients, you may want to have a folder or tray for each person.

As you become a better office organizer, you will want to maintain separate folders for each paperwork function such as paying bills, making calls, mailing forms, looking up on the Internet, and scheduling on the calendar. Even with ongoing and on-the-spot sorting, a few things will pile up in your receiving area for mail. The solution is to establish a particular time each week, say Saturday morning, for definitively disposing or filing anything that has piled up.

Filing Versus Piling. We have observed that people typically handle paper in one of two ways; either they create files or they build piles. When a filer (such as Mike) marries a piler (such as Betty) conflict can arise because the other doesn't appreciate the partner's method of organization. In our experience, you can be organized whether you prefer to file or pile—it just takes some effort with either method to stay current.

Files are particularly useful to avoid losing track of things and to organize a complex set of categories. Some people enjoy the scrapbook-like process of creating files, labeling them, and arranging folders in a cabinet drawer. For instance, it's often helpful to create a file folder for each type of bill you receive monthly, like water, gas, phone, electric, and major credit cards. Make other files for items you want to keep and access periodically, such as appliance instructions and documentation of your valuables. Tax files represent a category unto themselves. If you are a filer with a complex life, then you may need more than one filing cabinet.

Others prefer to create piles of paper. This method is particularly useful for short-term projects and long-term desktop organization. With piling, it's also easier to periodically trim away obsolete content. If you are comfortable with maintaining piles, then you will need a set of trays, shelves, or stackable boxes to hold your stacks. Containers for piling can be labeled, and it is best to have units of the same size to facilitate convenient handling of records and documents.

Labels Maintain the System. Once you have devised a system for how you will process paper, labeling can help you consistently implement your plan. You can create handwritten labels, but having a label maker will give you always-legible and sometimes professional-looking results. There are a variety of styles of label makers to consider based on your application. Brother p-touch label makers *http://www.brother-usa.com/ptouch/* and Dymo label makers *http://sites.dymo.com/ Pages/home.aspx?locale=enUS* work well. Labels will assist anywhere in your home to indicate where things are to be stored, and labels work especially well for paper files.

Computer Files. Electronic delivery of information has recently reduced the problem of paper clutter—but presents its own problems of organizing financial and other records. You might find it helpful to brush up on the function in your email system for creating files. Make it a regular practice to move email messages into these folders.

Many people use their email inbox as a kind of giant electronic piling area to accumulate the inflow of messages while saving the time required for filing. Because it's possible to search through one's inbox by means of keywords, large-scale electronic piles are certainly more efficient and useful than tall stacks of paper. Nevertheless, the people who send us email frequently fail to post a truly informative subject heading. In addition, people often reuse old emails as a basis for new ones. All of this means that a keyword search of the inbox may gradually become less effective for locating particular messages.

Some email systems allow you to create sorting rules based on the sender of the message, or based on key words in the title, to automatically move an incoming message to an electronic folder. Other systems create a portal so that all of your information resides in the cloud. The idea here is to access your personal records with your password at your convenience.

And again we make the point that electronics have not completely displaced paper. Fully 51% of office workers still have paper files at their desk according to a study conducted between May 19 and June 8, 2011 by Harris Interactive.[4] Some people seem better able to organize paper files than computer files—and vice versa. Try to work on one format, say the paper files, till you are satisfied, and then see if you can apply what you've learned from that plan to organize the other filing format.

We also strongly recommend that you periodically purge paper and computer files to ferret out dated material. We do this annually as part of our tax-paying ritual. When we've completed our taxes for the current year, we file those records that are important for tax documentation and long-term retention. Almost everything else—notably, monthly bills—gets purged to make way for the new inflow of paper.

Bill Paying and Finance

The home-office or home-desk area is usually where we keep track of money matters. What's needed is a place of reasonable privacy where we won't be disturbed. Some people do most of their bill-paying and other financial work on computer; but it is likely that a certain amount of paper processing continues to be required.

Bill Paying. Most banks now offer an automatic bill-paying option that can simplify paperwork and check writing. Institutions frequently push this option because it saves them the cost of mailing and cuts down on the amount of paper they have to produce. If you don't already have your routine bills on automatic bill pay, consider this option.

Financial Records. Once bills are paid, you need to have a system for storing records. Financial paperwork such as bank statements and monthly bills need to be processed and then appropriately filed. Suze Orman has a useful list of what records to store and for how long at *http://www.suzeorman.com/igsbase/igstemplate. cfm?SRC=DB&SRCN=&GnavID=84&SnavID=152&TnavID*. Keep a file folder, electronically or in hard copy—or both—for each account where you have paid a bill. You will want to purge most of these monthly statements at the end of the tax year—although retaining certain receipts of major purchases that may relate to warranties or to keeping track of the basis of an owned residence. It's also good to keep records of payments for a year or so because such statements often contain important telephone numbers and contact information—all useful for follow-up with regards to service.

If you don't maintain a bank safe deposit box, the office area becomes the go-to site for storing particularly important papers such as birth certificates, passports, marriage licenses, car titles, deeds to major assets, and so on. Office supply stores frequently carry inexpensive fireproof safes or strong boxes. Fire departments recommend that the safe be able to withstand heat up to 1700 F for at least two hours and be waterproof.

Although everyone needs to keep track of and store crucial financial paperwork—notably, those pertaining to property and investments—it remains the case that financial records need to be purged periodically. Fortunately, getting rid of financial records has never been easier because banks and investment firms now make historical service-account and investment records available online. Here it's important for you to check how long the information will be accessible in electronic form and make appropriate paper or electronic copies of any critical information that you will need for the long haul.

Keeping tax records presents a more specialized problem because the taxpayer is subject to specific IRS and state rules and guidelines. The standard tax advice is to retain permanently every year's basic tax return document (such as the Form 1040 and related schedules), but to keep the supporting information (such as receipts and financial 1099s) for seven years. For questions, the IRS has a website *www.irs.gov*. It needs be remembered that while the tax exemptions and deductions you claim are subject to being overruled—with or without penalty—more serious consequences result from failure to file an income tax return. Also it needs be noted that failure to report income is considered to be fraud with no statute of limitation.

Documentation relating to the tax basis (i.e., original and cumulative costs) of assets should be kept for as long as you own the asset—plus seven years after its sale if you will owe tax on the gain or loss. Assets in this category would be stocks and bonds, your home, investment real estate or partnerships. When you sell the asset, you will calculate your gain based on the sales price minus the purchase price combined with any cost increases. These increases include (1) improvements made to your home (or investment real estate), (2) deposits or reinvestments in a financial instrument, or (3) allowable expenses incurred such as legal advice or a financial transaction fee. Remember that anything related to adjusting the cost basis of a taxable asset or investment needs be documented and retained for the duration of your ownership—and seven years beyond.

Health Documents and Wills

As with important financial records, our health history needs to be documented and maintained for access. Naturally, you'll have one or more paper files for medical records. However, medical information systems are emerging that will enable us to keep most all of our health-related information conveniently in an electronic form. Some hospitals already offer this service to their patients using a consolidated data base of their health histories, drug allergies, test results, and hospitalizations. Even when widespread access to such systems becomes commonplace, it will still be good to for you to file paperwork that is received pertaining to family medical conditions.

File your medical paperwork with this question in mind: What would you need to lay your hands on if a health crisis unfolded in your home or if you received news about a family member's emergency? Here you would likely need insurance papers, personal health data (immunizations, allergies), and key contacts for medical providers including telephone numbers and email/ web addresses. Create a file or files with copies of this information and make it accessible enough to be moved quickly. Create an entry on your mobile phone labeled ICE, "in case of emergency," where you store key contact information.

By definition, health emergencies are unpredictable—and this means they may happen to anyone in the family, parents as well as children. So it makes sense to alert members of your family, those of sufficient age, to the whereabouts of key medical documentation. In addition, parents and grandparents are well advised to have prepared a living will (that specifies the particulars of medical treatments and resuscitation) and a durable power of attorney. This POA would be a document authorizing a person or persons to make medical and financial decisions in the event a designated person becomes incapacitated.

Software tools can help you organize your will and health documents and store them electronically. Care Binders Software *www.carebinders.com* enables you to scan important documents and backup onto a flash drive. You could carry the flash drive with you on your key ring to keep copies of important papers with you at all times. Legacies and Lifelines *http://www.legaciesandlifelines.com/* offers solutions for optimal later-life living, including vehicles for communicating with caregivers and important information about your history. Organize the Essentials *http://organizetheessentials.com/* provides a method to keep your entire health documents ready in case of emergency by means of a variety of wristbands or special containers.

BEDROOMS AND CLOTHES CLOSETS

Rest is the natural follow-up to activity— and the Stuff Cure applies to bedrooms as well to home offices. Begin by visualizing how your bedroom might look if it were to be featured in an ad for a getaway hotel. You never see these places crowded with stuff. Instead, we are treated to a beautiful

> "A place for everything, everything in its place."
>
> Benjamin Franklin,
> Poor Richard's Almanac

panorama—a romantic setting enmeshed in a relaxed environment. Masters of feng shui (the Asian art of arrangement and decoration) believe a couple will become closer if they keep the area around the bed free from clutter.[5]

You'll be happier with your sleep quarters if you are able to use the room without shoes and clothing strewn about and with only your daily-use items on chest and night table. Begin by assessing everything that you have on top of bedroom furniture. Find a place in drawers, cabinets, shelves, or the closet for anything for which you have only occasional need.

The next step is to take stock of what comes into the bedroom on a daily basis; and this step will find you assessing not only the furniture but also the closet. Bedroom closets represent the ideal location for the range of daily-use items. While closets are usually designed with shoes and clothing in mind, you may be able to carve out a spot or two for storage boxes in which excess knickknacks can be located. Here you could box up items such as jewelry that you use only occasionally. Remember that things boxed and unused are candidates for periodic unstuffing.

Upper shelves in a closet are ideal for items that are easily lifted up high such as extra sheets and blankets. However, bed linen and towels consume enough space that you might want to consider storing these items in a blanket chest at the foot of the bed or in an under-bed drawer. In either case, you could place a folded set of sheets inside one of the pillowcases to keep the set together.

Clothes

Our clothing usually represents the greatest source of closet clutter; we're all just too likely to hang onto old favorites that we no longer wear for reasons of size, style, or condition. Periodically assess your clothes with focus on shoes that no longer fit, pants or jackets that aren't comfortable to wear, or tops that are out of style.

The website Six Items or Less *www.sixitemsorless.com* once challenged women to go for one month wearing only six items already found in their closet—not counting shoes, underwear, or accessories. Participants said they were motivated to take the challenge for reasons that included: (1) a way to trim their spending, (2) an outright rejection of trendiness, and (3) a concern that the mass production and global transportation of clothing damaged the environment. Many participants enjoyed success, and some described the experience as liberating.[6] Imagine how easy it would be to organize your closet if you focused attention on a relatively few things frequently worn.

In addition to periodic reassessments of the wardrobe, closet organization also enables us to get more utility out of clothing. Some people arrange clothes by type—shirts, jackets, pants, and skirts—while others group by color or outfits. In any case, try to position your clothes in a way that alerts you to possible combinations or different outfits.

People who group by color often separate garments into two lengths—full length and half length. Within each length, it's good to arrange by color in the following sequence: white, cream, yellow, orange, pink, red, purple, blue, green, brown, and black. Within each color, go light to dark. Prints can be placed with the predominate colors in the print, or all can be placed together in the center of the sequence. If you have a matching jacket and skirt/pants, they will be placed next to one another using this method. Having chosen a skirt or pants, you can choose a top in a complementary color.

In addition to grouping clothes by type and color, some people use a rotation system to help them vary what they wear. For example, for clothes hung on the rod, they take out items from the right side of the rod and return them to the left side of the rod. By analogy, clean clothes also may be hung on the left side of the rod. In any case, clothes that persistently linger on the right side of the rod would be candidates for unstuffing.

Closet Organization Systems

Once you have pared down and optimally hung your wardrobe, modern closet systems offer additional help. Advertisements for these systems often include a "before" picture that shows a single rod and piles of clutter on the floor. The "after" picture depicts a closet complete with shelves, drawers, and rods—all perfectly occupying the closet's horizontal and vertical space—with everything either neatly hung or folded. A closet system cannot replace periodic unstuffing, but it can help you maximize capacity. You may want to look at California Closets *www.californiaclosets.com*, Elfa *www.elfa.com*, and Ikea *www.ikea.com*.

Closet organization also includes having the right type and number of hangers. Just a bit of checking will alert you to special hangers for pants, skirts, scarves, neckties, and belts; these are available in most home stores. Got bow ties? A customized hanger can be ordered from Beau Ties *www.beautiesltd.com*.

Even where you have a chest of drawers, you may want to take advantage of closet-based units including stackable pull-out drawer units, basket systems, or canvas drawer systems. The Container Store *http://www.containerstore.com/shop/storage/drawers* and Target *www.target.com* offer nice choices for drawer units. Stackable drawers provide a lot of flexibility such that you may find them useful in a range of locations in your home. You might pick up a set for that new high-school graduate because they are a perennial favorite for college dorm rooms.

It's useful to consider how the closet figures into the laundering process. Everyone needs some kind of hamper for dirty clothes and for items earmarked for the dry cleaner. Instead of one giant bin, consider two smaller ones—that is, separate bins for light and dark colors. This not only saves time in sorting but also helps you set laundry priorities. Put aside any items marred by difficult stains or that require some kind of sewing repair. If your set-aside place is off the beaten path, be sure to make a note of clothing placed there so that you'll either fix the problem or include the item in your periodic review.

A judicious combination of periodic reassessment and systemizing will usually solve problems of clothing clutter. Particularly if you're doing other remodeling, however, you may also want to have a carpenter review your closet for the possible addition of shelves and rods in your closet. Have your remodeler also advise you about whether a nearby electrical receptacle may be tapped to enhance closet lighting. Everything is easier when you can actually see what you're doing.

Shoes

The shoe collections of Philippine first lady Imelda Marcos and Ponzi-scammer Bernie Madoff are legendary. And shoe mania was a regular theme on the "Sex and the City" TV series and movies. All this suggests that probably we all are keeping more pairs than are really needed. After all, shoe styles change each year. Moreover, the addition of new shoes can give an old outfit a new look. While some styles are classic, it's often the case that old shoes just look like old shoes.

Effectively organizing shoes helps not only with respect to style but also to time. This often-ignored savings of time was dramatically demonstrated in a survey conducted by IKEA, the home-furnishings retailer. Under the banner of "You Can't Be Too Organized," the folks at IKEA questioned 620 randomly chosen individuals, finding that "women with shoe racks were seven times more likely to be on time for work that women without shoe racks."[7]

For reasons of care as well as organization, it repays to store shoes in their original boxes, on shoe racks, in clear plastic shoe boxes, or in a shoe holder that can be hung from the closet rod or over the back of the door. For men, the original-box method probably is all that is required—but for higher quality leather shoes it is always well to place shoe trees (cedar wood ones are best) inside to ensure that footwear retains its proper shape.

It is sometimes the case that home flooring needs protection from shoes. In many cultures it's common to remove shoes worn on the street and, in the home, replace them with sandals. Such a custom occasionally emerges in families where a premium is placed on protecting a white carpet or new wood flooring—or in resort areas where gritty sand is frequently tracked in. If any of these purposes fits your own family's needs, consider setting aside a spot for a shoe cabinet by the door.

Jewelry

Forms of jewelry have been found in cave dwellings dating to 40,000 years ago. As a beloved form of personal adornment, jewelry can express emotion, romance, happiness, and beauty; associated deeper meanings relate to status, magic, religion, or group membership. From the standpoint of space consumed, jewelry may not be your biggest stuff concern, but a plan for storing and organizing it nevertheless will add value. Elizabeth Taylor certainly believed this to be true. She devoted the entire second floor of her California home to the storage of her jewelry and clothes.[8] Most of us don't enjoy million-dollar collections of necklaces, rings, or cuff links; but everyone benefits from keeping accessories organized, accessible, and safe.

Jewelry can be organized by type of piece. For women, rings in one place, necklaces in another, and earrings on their own rack. For men, a single cigar-box-sized container typically suffices for cufflinks, tuxedo-shirt studs, and the like. Women frequently own enough fashion accessories to organize them by color— red pieces, green pieces, silver, and gold. Larger collections benefit from the purchase of attractive jewelry boxes or mini-armoires—or from partitions slipped inside dresser drawers. Some women prefer to have a peg or cork board with hooks so that they can peruse necklaces in one glance.

It's important to store high-value pieces to protect them from inadvertent loss or damage. Here it is good to maintain a household file for information that documents the purchase, provenance of manufacture, and any care instructions. For family heirlooms, include notes about when you first remember seeing the item in the family home and any associated story.

When your jewelry items are really valuable, you may want the additional protection of insurance. Remember that standard homeowners or renters insurance rarely provides anything more than minimal protection. Ask your insurance agent about the treatment of high-value items. In this connection, you will need to itemize anything to be included—and it helps to take pictures of each item in addition to any documented appraisals.

BATHROOMS FOR HYGIENE AND BEAUTY

The cultural role of the bathroom continues to increase from the days when simple indoor plumbing was sufficient and from the post-WWII standard of three bedrooms/one bath. In new construction, it's not uncommon for a house to have more bathrooms than bedrooms. And the spa-like architecture of contemporary bathrooms virtually demands an extensive array of towels, treatments, shampoos, and potions. Before emerging into the world, we turn to our collection of cosmetics to finish our face and hair. Even men have gotten into the game with shaving systems that include razor, razor-stand, brush, cream, lubricating oil, and finishing balm.

Patent and Prescription Medicines

The Stuff-Cure approach to organizing a bathroom begins with your using up inventories of excess soaps, shampoos, lotions, and creams—and your keeping just the currently used items close to the sink.

It's amazing how long old bathroom supplies can linger if left undisturbed in a cabinet or drawer. Mike once found a box of dental floss in his parents' guest bathroom that was so old that the manufacturer's address lacked a zip code—meaning that it was packaged before 1964. Particularly for pain relievers, sunscreens, and antiseptics, regularly review whether bottles and tubes are within the recommended time frame.

With respect to prescription medicines, insurance companies increasingly favor online or mail-order pharmacies. The result is that we often are sent three-month's worth of prescriptions—requiring that we find a dry and accessible storage solution. If your bathroom is cramped, consider designating a clear plastic storage box in the bedroom closet as the go-to site for back-up supplies. Cold medicines and other relatively seasonal items (mosquito repellent, et cetera) can also be stored in this location. When medicines have expired, be sure to put them in the trash rather than flushing them down the toilet and polluting the water supply.

Bathroom Linen

Unless your home is new or custom built, it's likely that your bathrooms may be somewhat undersized, lacking in built-in towel bars, and/or minus a sufficient number of shelves.

It's easier to keep bathroom linen off the floor if you have a sufficient number of towel bars. Home-improvement stores carry easy-to-install towel racks that are perfect for otherwise useless spaces, such as the side of the vanity or over the toilet. It's also possible to purchase a dual-function standing towel rack and warmer. You can find towel warmers at the Towel Warmer Store *http://www.towelwarmerstore.com* and My Sonic *http://www.mysoninc.com*.

If your bathroom lacks built-in shelving or cabinet space, you may take advantage of rubber or plastic stackable storage boxes or drawers in the smaller sizes. In your search of the local home store and online, you may also find specialized storage equipment such as the hair dryer caddy offered by Crate and Barrel *http://www. crateandbarrel.com/bed-and-bath/bath-accessories/style-station/s372440*.

Cosmetics

The first archaelogical evidence of cosmetics usage was found in Egypt from around 3500 BCE.[9] Talk about expiration dates!

Cosmetics are not only most effective but also most hygienic when they are fresh. Eye makeup, for example, should only be kept for about six months. Several cosmetics now carry a symbol of an open jar with a number signifying the number of months that you should keep the product after opening it. Old cosmetics risk microbial growth that could cause problems when applied to your skin.

Keep one area for your cosmetics for your everyday look, another area for your every-night treatments, and a third area for evening or special occasions. Keep only those shades that are most flattering to you. If you like to buy cosmetics that give free samples, find a friend who looks good in the shades that don't look good on you and exchange the samples while they are still fresh.

CHILDREN'S BEDROOMS

Newer, larger homes enable individual members of the family to have their own personal room. Children's stuff mounts up—even when they're still in diapers. At the time of a family move to a new house, a time when our boys had outgrown things of the under-two-years-old set, we found ourselves gifting, trading, or donating several moving boxes worth of toddler goods.

Kid's Stuff

As they grow, children continue to be magnets for stuff—toys for different ages, endless school things, trophies, certificates, uniforms, sports equipment, clothes, and shoes.

Stuff clings to kids, too. Even at the age of three, our youngest had amassed quite a collection of bright and smooth rocks that he'd found in playgrounds and parks—all of which were precious to him. This means that it's important to help your youngsters develop habits of responsibly moving stuff along. Outfit their room with storage shelves and bins at a level where they can put things away. When the amount of stuff exceeds the capacity of the containers, help your children prune out some of the things not currently being used. Create a box for excess items that can go in your storage room or Stuff-Cure staging area. Don't forget to consult with your children before actually disposing of anything!

Toys

Toys represent a category that expands exponentially. Parents can extend the play value of toys by collecting up items that have fallen by the wayside and then bringing them out again, later. The old stuff takes on the aura of something new and exciting. In relation to unstuffing playthings, parents can take advantage of the fact that, as children grow, certain toys take on a negative connotation as something for younger ages. Children are also more willing to part with toys in a context where they can still play with them occasionally. When our boys were three and five, we gathered up and donated over five medium sized boxes of old baby toys to their daycare center. The same principle would apply to placing old toys with Sunday schools, relatives, or younger neighborhood friends.

Toys for children older than three all seem to be designed with small component parts. Over time, parents develop a sixth sense for walking around the room and not stepping on and breaking small pieces. Here a possible help would be a special storage container, called Box 4 Blox *www.box4blox.com* that contains four trays with different sized grids. You put the blocks, such as Legos, in the top tray and then shake. The blocks fall through the holes and are sorted by size into four separate trays. The most troublesome tiny pieces end up in the bottom tray.

Nevertheless, it's often the case that small component parts stay hidden until it's time to clean the house or move furniture. Some do not reappear until the movers appear to load up the van. When vacating the house where our boys grew up, we came upon many long-lost projectiles belonging to various Nerf guns along with quarter-sized disks from the boys' Teenage Mutant Ninja Turtles pizza-firing machine.

Artwork

From the time of preschool, children come home with various papers and artwork. What parent doesn't want to affirm children's artistic skill and imagination by displaying these productions on refrigerator or wall? Our earliest success in getting a handle on this artistic inflow was to designate a push-pin bulletin board expressly for posting children's artwork. As the older artwork became covered by the new, we gradually removed the older pieces to a storage box. Later we sorted the artwork, dispensing with some of it.

The Stuff-Cure criterion of "outrageously sentimental" most likely applies to a relatively few items such as children's handcrafted Mother's Day cards. These are the prime candidates to be dated and filed away. In any case, all children's art work to be kept should be labeled with the child's name and the date when created. You can also turn your child's art into a coffee table book at Souvenart Books *http://www.souvenartebooks.com/*.

Tips to Help Kids Curb Clutter

Involve your kids in keeping their own rooms in order. Kathy Peel suggests five "room rules" to keep the clutter in their rooms under control.[10]

1. Do not take food into bedrooms.
2. Place all dirty clothes in a basket or hamper daily.
3. Do not leave potentially dangerous items, such as balls, plastic building pieces, and roller skates on the floor.
4. Put away toys no longer being played with before getting out something new.
5. Straighten up the room before going to bed.

STORAGE, TOOLS, AND CAR

The Stuff Cure applies to attics, basements, and the garage as well as to the more visible and public places in the house. Less elegant regions of the residence become important components of the Stuff Cure by serving as permanent storage areas. Also they can house the Staging Area that, as seen in Chapter 6, is essential to the Stuff Cure method.

Attic/Basement

Basements and attics are often a challenge to organize because they are filled with items that need to be unstuffed. Things frequently migrate to basement or attic because we don't have time to store them properly, because they are broken and await future repair, or because we are keeping them as a hedge against future needs. So it repays to periodically stroll (or climb) through basement and attic with the principles of the Stuff Cure in mind.

Seasonal Use and Sports Equipment. It's a good home-organizational policy to designate specific storage locations for seasonal-use and occasional-use items. These would include suitcases, sports and camping equipment, heavy winter clothing, and holiday decorations. Invest in some vertical shelving to keep items off the floor and in clear view. You'll find that storage systems and units designed for the garage can also be adapted to attic or basement. Remember that the best storage environment is a place out of direct sunlight, with a temperature of 68 degrees, and with 40 to 50 percent humidity.

Holiday Decorations. After the holidays, put in storage only those things you really enjoyed during the season. It's useful to clearly label the season—Halloween, Thanksgiving, Christmas—and the contents of each box. If you like to save paper and bows for reuse, make sure that they are stored in a dry place as the colors can run if they get wet. If an item stays unused for more than one season, then consider unstuffing.

Staging Area. Ideal places for a Stuff-Cure staging area would be a floor-area spot next to the basement stairs, a space just inside the attic door, or a broad shelf in a corner of the garage or laundry room. Here it's possible to make storing less boring by locating your unstuffing headquarters at the primary site of the clutter problem.

Workshop

The workshop and the tool shed are the natural centers for do-it-yourself activity. All too often we assume that these spaces—usually maintained by the man of the house—are by their very nature, messy. But it's possible to treat these work areas with as much pride and care as any other room in the residence.

Tools. The right tools, properly maintained, are crucial for successful do-it–yourself projects. If you're lucky, you'll have built-in cabinets and drawers. In any case, it's always a good idea to set up some kind of workbench and accentuate it with peg board and hooks to permit easy access to hammers and other tools. Four-foot by eight-foot sheets of peg board are easily obtained at lumberyards or big-box remodeling stores.

In the absence of built-ins, plastic storage boxes are useful for such basic hand tools as wrenches, knives, files, clamps, drill bits, et cetera. For boxes containing metal tools, it's good to toss in one or two packs of moisture-absorbing desiccants that come with electronics or vitamin-pill bottles. It's best to keep nails and screws in their original containers and store them in a larger plastic container. Nevertheless, you'll find that miscellaneous small parts mount up, and for storing them, nothing beats plastic peanut butter jars. To save trips to and fro, it's good to have a portable toolkit containing such basics as hammer, screwdrivers, duct tape, power drill, picture hooks, etc.

Painting Equipment. No category of do-it-yourselfing pays greater dividends than painting. To be sure, the first four letters of the word "paint" spell "pain"—making the word somewhat off putting on a psychological basis. Nevertheless, for reasons of both savings and satisfaction, it is useful to hone skills for wall preparation and painting. The basic requisites are relatively few: high-quality brushes for reuse; cheap brushes for one-use projects; paint rollers and trays; stirring sticks; patching paste; putty knives; sandpaper; masking tape.

It used to be the case that oil-based paints required messy and smelly clean-up with paint thinner or turpentine. With today's latex paints and stains, it's very easy to become adept at finishing walls, decks, and fences. Even when you've hired a professional painter, you'll find yourself wanting to store extra paint for touch-up jobs. Make sure that these paint cans are sealed tightly, are labeled (as to date, color, and location), are kept away from water and heat, and are stored such that they are not liable to tipping over. Be sure to keep close review of your paints and dispose of obsolete cans properly—that is, not in the regular trash. It's likely that your locality has some recycling center for hazardous liquids. Our Monterey, California waste-management facility accepts cans of old paint and makes them available to others for free.

Garage

Garages represent a metric for success in the Stuff Cure because keeping cars in the garage every night represents a key goal in the crusade against clutter. Evidence that this objective can be significant comes from data showing that a majority of people with two-car garages are unable to find a place there for both cars. In addition, 25 percent of all homeowners don't park any cars in their garages.[11]

Start the task of organizing the garage on a nice day so you can put things in the driveway while you're working. Space near the top of the garage usefully invites hooks for hanging bicycles or shelves for items seldom accessed. Items stored in the garage are often quite heavy, so make sure any storage units or brackets are securely installed and will hold the weight that you intend. One brand of garage storage systems can be found at Monkey Bar Storage *www.MonkeyBarStorage.com*.

It's possible to install shelves at the front of the garage that extend over the hood of the car when the vehicle is parked. Place these front shelves or cabinets at least 51 inches from the floor, the maximum height for the hood of most cars. Most garages regularly take in moisture from cars coming and going in times of rain or snow. Try to keep everything off the floor of the garage where moisture and dirt can accumulate.

Automotive. Auto-related equipment can be interspersed with other handyman items in a work-bench area. Auto fluids such as or oil, antifreeze, and wiper fluid can be stored with cleaning fluids or paint-related items.

It's good to keep basic emergency road supplies in the trunk of your car. In case of trouble, you'll be glad you have packed an ice scraper, flashlight, bicycle foot pump, jumper cables, toolset, roll of wire, duct tape, and some gloves.

Yard. Wall hooks and large plastic bins are ideal for most of the major lawn-and-garden-care tools. Lawn mowers are notorious space hogs. So, before you put them away, be sure that you do some basic clean-up—especially at the end of the season. Try to not bring yard waste into the garage as that can result in a condition known as "halitosis of the garage" or "garagitosis."

THE RIGHT STUFF IN THE RIGHT PLACE

"A place for everything, everything in its place" represents a familiar American saying, originally printed in Benjamin Franklin's *Poor Richard's Almanac*. As we take on more responsibilities and acquire more assets, we need to become better organized to deal with it all. Let's face it, sometimes we have to ramp up our home management just to find the car keys! That's why we've focused this chapter on a room-by-room approach to organization and stuff outflow.

However difficult it is to get organized—it's harder to stay so. From TV shows about extreme home makeovers, we observe that home owners tend to return to their old habits soon after the organizing team has left. In this chapter, we've observed where certain aspects of a clutter emergency can be solved by commercial organizing systems. You can find organizing products for every room in your home—available at a wide range of stores and on the Internet. For instance, Organized A to Z *http://www.organizedatoz.com/* sells bins, baskets, storage systems, under-bed boxes, hangers and racks; and all of these are endorsed by professional organizers. You may also want to check out three additional sites: Target *www.target.com*; Organize *www.organize.com*; and Container Store *www.containerstore.com*.

Organizing systems are a help; but if you've followed our story up to this point in the book, you know that the Stuff Cure relies less on storage systems and more on new attitudes and behaviors that bring us to the sources of clutter. In our next chapter—"Doing It Unstuffed"— we elaborate on ways to make the Stuff Cure a lasting part of your life.

• thestuffcure •

8

DOING IT UNSTUFFED

Grandpa John was a child of that generation coming to maturity in the Great Depression. After the family ranching business went bankrupt in the early 1930s, John lived with his mother and brother in a sparse two-room cabin situated on a 30-acre plot alongside the beautiful Wind River near Riverton, Wyoming. Growing up with few personal possessions, John, as he prospered from a career in electrical engineering, enjoyed acquiring things. The large Victorian home that John shared in Ohio with his wife, Kay, overflowed with the fruits of his hobby of attending local estate sales. In the public rooms, one would find the walls crowded with framed artwork. Shelf after shelf, and cabinet after cabinet, brimmed with china and glass decorations. Upstairs could be seen such collections as a nearly complete set of *National Geographic* magazines dating from the 1890s.

Grandpa John's auctioneering specialty was bidding on boxes of miscellaneous goods—all the better if they contained broken things that could be repaired. His workshop was a bastion of projects completed and half-completed. In organizing and storing spare parts for future repairs and crafts, John discovered the science of storage containers long before the age of plastic. He regularly cleaned out glass baby-food jars and peanut-butter jars which he combined with hundreds of empty paper cigar boxes supplied to him by a friend at the local drugstore. At one point, he even stored his extra boxes of spares in a friend's garage attic.

From a lifetime habit of accumulation in successively larger houses, John and Kay eventually amassed an inventory of possessions that, at the time of their move to a smaller home, filled four of the largest available moving vans. One of these behemoths transported furniture and other contents to their new home in Nevada; two vans-full of surplus were disposed of in a large estate sale; and one van transported donations to Saint Vincent De Paul.

Stuff-Cure living came late to Grandpa John. But he approached the Life With Less in the same engineering spirit that, earlier, he had applied to accumulation. Motivated by a desire of not burdening his children, John gradually worked through his remaining extras that now were piled to the ceiling in half of a two-car garage. Patiently he sorted through his collections of picture frames, antique wooden tools, colorful glassware, and the like—disposing of them through gifts, donations, and at "Lightning's Auctions," a favorite consignment house.

Even as he downsized, however, Grandpa John's love of collecting never entirely went away. But gradually he came upon a way of collecting that did not result in a major physical accumulation. One of his new-style collections came in the form of license plate sightings. John would note, and later write down, unusual vanity-plate licenses that he saw, penciling in the state of issue, and sometimes such other details as the make of the car. Eventually, John's family and friends would gift him with rosters of their own vanity-tag sightings. Reading these lists aloud always produced a good laugh. John had happened upon a kind of collecting that didn't cost any money to acquire, didn't take any room to store, and created fun and interaction with friends and family.

Grandpa John's conversion to downsizing and spaceless collecting didn't come into play until he had reached his seventies. In contrast, the Stuff Cure is all about making this transformation before it is pressed upon us by circumstances of smaller residences or greater age. In this chapter, we address some of the biggest challenges in moving forward with an Unstuffed Life. We'll share our solutions for leaner forms of gift giving, gift receiving, shopping, and collecting. Our focus will be on life after the Cure and making the Cure last whatever our stage in life.

GIVING MORE WITH LESS

Gift giving represents a constant source of new stuff. Designer Hubert Givenchy once sent actress Audrey Hepburn fifty rose bushes on her fiftieth birthday.[1] We'll hope that her home came complete with sufficient yard and with a groundskeeper ready to plant the bushes. A bouquet of fifty roses might have been an equally lovely gift, something not necessitating planting and ongoing tending.

Let's take a look at several categories of gifts that convey powerful sentiment without increasing someone's inventory of stuff.

Inedible Perishables

Mike's mother, Kay, used to ask for gifts of "inedible perishables." By that she meant things that were enjoyable but that didn't last forever. Kay didn't want edible perishables as she was always concerned about calories. It proved to be fun to find birthday and holiday gifts that fit into the category of inedible perishables. What we settled upon included fresh flowers, note cards, fancy paper napkins, or theater tickets.

Concert and event tickets can become very memorable and exciting gifts if we calibrate them carefully to the interests of our family and friends. In addition to the experience itself, recipients enjoy anticipating the event and then remembering.

Media-related gifts also share the two qualities of having an impact while being expendable. Stamps, envelopes, and stationary are useful additions to the home office for people who like to write letters. Prepaid phone cards work for people who prefer conversation. An app for the smart phone can be tailored to a person's particular interests. The same holds for gift cards for golfing-green fees and certificates for pedicures or massages.

Possessionless Gifts

The power of a gift extends beyond its cost. Research on married couples done at the Institute for Social Research at the University of Michigan indicates that "romance and passion are all about using the elements of surprise and the elements of newness."[2] Practice that kind of generous giving which foregrounds thoughtfulness, loving sentiments, and appropriate gestures as you pursue deep connection and emotion in your relationships. You may very well find out that such giving doesn't produce as much stuff.

To celebrate our 36th anniversary, Mike gave Betty a "big rock." Being a good recipient of the surprising gift, Betty was happy not to actually own the rock; the boulder in question surfaces in the Monterey Bay every morning for viewing from the living room window. Mike's inscribed gift card was attached to the window with a "rock viewing" aperture such that the stone was featured for visual admiration. We now call it our "anniversary rock"—and we didn't have to buy it, don't have to dust it, and need not worry about its being stolen or lost.

"Anniversary rock" illustrates how intangible gifts can become significant along the lines of verbal sentiments or meaningful action. Taking the idea of the intangible gift even further are Charlie Turpin and his wife, Jewell, who have been married 56 years. Mr. Turpin describes standard gift-giving as something they have outgrown. "It really is liberating," he said noting the stress that came from needing to read one another's mind on command because of a mark on the calendar. "Early in life, presents and occasions are important, but as you get older, you have everything you want."[3]

The Perfect Gift

The *Ladies Home Journal* in 1912 suggested gifts of money for Christmas because a cash gift "supplies dearly cherished wishes, adds small luxuries, prevents worriment and gives opportunities for helpfulness as no other gift does."[4] This example speaks against what is often presented as a "traditional" assumption that cash represents laziness or crassness on the part of the giver. In this present day, when so much is done online or in virtual reality, cash no longer represents something alien from a lived environment. In the digital age, available money constitutes the ultimate inedible perishable.

Much of gift giving lies in the art of presentation—and this applies to cash as well as to commodities. Some nice crisp bills, perhaps given in a red envelope as in the Chinese custom, signals care on the part of the giver and offers the recipient complete flexibility. If you want to get creative, you might fashion the bills into something like a ring, a corsage, or a money tree. Another approach is to wrap up the money in some kind of way that will trigger a shared memory or reflects a timely situation. If you transfer stock as a gift, often the brokerage house has a lovely certificate announcing the transfer. In any event, no cash gift should come without the gift-giver's expressing written or televisual communication that references shared experiences, memories, or anecdotes.

Cash gifts can also be earmarked to a charity or cause that you know the recipient supports. Many organizations are prepared to send out gift-in-honor announcements and may otherwise publicize memorial gifts by means of a publication or an invitation to an annual reception. Separate from any institutional acknowledgment, you should send your own personalized sentiments to the recipient. Donation gifts are most suitable when the amount exceeds what would be expected in a direct cash gift for the particular kind of occasion.

> "Simplicity is the ultimate sophistication."
>
> *Leonardo da Vinci, Italian Painter, Sculptor, and Architect*

MORE SHOPPING, LESS BAGGAGE

When we celebrated our 33rd wedding anniversary, Mike wanted to give Betty an emerald ring—her favorite stone. But knowing that Betty likes to pick out her jewelry, Mike wrote down the promise of the gift in the anniversary card. For several months afterward, we had lots of fun shopping in local jewelry stores and while on vacation. Eighteen months later, while on a trip to Providence, Rhode Island, we found just the right ring.

Betty's anniversary ring resulted, eventually, in a purchase; but the point we are emphasizing is the total experience. Not only does Betty enjoy owning her anniversary emerald, but she carries in memory receiving the hand-written note promising the ring, the sights and conversations associated with the shopping, and the particular occasion of purchase. Everything culminated to enhance the outrageously sentimental nature of this anniversary remembrance.

Shopping for the Experience of It

Betty's emerald story shows that a lot of the pleasure of shopping is separate from actual acquisition. Stuffless shopping represents a focus on observing and learning—with ownership as a possible but deemphasized objective. It's like going to a museum, except there are price tags attached to the items on view. The idea is to savor the hunt rather than the trophies.

See how many times you can take a shopping trip without bringing back bags. If you like antiques, for example, part of the fun would be to increase your knowledge of certain categories of things, say Wedgwood china and earthenware. Wedgewood represents a recognizable category that, if you didn't see anything, you could inquire about. Your educational orientation would be the entry point for stimulating conversations with experts about some of your favorite collectables.

Enjoying Stuffless Shopping

Experience-based shopping represents an effort to recreate the small-town ambience of friendly conversation. This orientation works best when we are patronizing smaller shops where we may encounter the owner rather than in big-box stores that emphasize low price over value-added information.

The following guidelines will help you enjoy shopping that does not result in a purchase:
1. Let conversations with shopkeepers unfold naturally; approach shopkeepers only when they seem open to a bit of chitchat.
2. Remember that experience-based shopping is relationship building—so when you go out to buy, do patronize stores where you like to browse.
3. Don't pester the shopkeeper or keep him or her from other clients.
4. Minimize handling merchandise—this takes up the shopkeeper's time and increases your risk.
5. Don't ask to see items behind a counter—unless you actually have in mind to buy.
6. Don't make disparaging comments about merchandise—the idea is that everyone has a pleasant time.
7. Turn off your cell phone while in the store—and don't use the shop as a site for a lengthy unrelated conversation with a friend.
8. Don't leave a child unattended.

A final plus of stuffless shopping: you're much less likely to regret a purchase and find yourself in the returns line.

COLLECTING WITH LESS

If you think a bit about what collecting means, it doesn't necessarily require more stuff. In our standard home dictionary, the first entry for "collection" is "the act or process of collecting"; only in the second definition do we find mention of "things collected." Let's reflect on this.

Collecting Experiences

Many people have already learned to collect experiences rather than things. We know lots of people who like to travel and post their pictures and comments on their experiences on Facebook *www.Facebook.com* or in a blog. We also know people who collect annual experiences, like being a regular at Ohio State football games, the San Francisco Antiquarian Book Fair, or the Monterey Jazz Festival. We know sports fans who collect opportunities to go to the World Series or to visit every major league baseball stadium. Enthusiasts for coastal America build vacations around visiting scenic lighthouses, and hikers like to log miles on sections of the Appalachian Trail. Right now, you may be saying to yourself—but what about the gift shops at these places! So let's continue.

Collecting through Notes and Pictures

It's likely that our major league baseball fans have held onto their various ticket stubs and maybe a program or two. This is in the direction of minimalist collecting focused most directly on the experience.

Consider the case of Thomas Jefferson. Gardening was one of his many interests. In his journal, he kept careful notes of what he planted, when trees and bushes bore fruit, and details about each particular growing season. From his documented experiences, Jefferson learned to become a better gardener. He even organized competitions with his neighbors concerning who would produce the first green peas each season.[5]

Before radio and television, people often kept what was called a commonplace book where they would record their observations and experiences. This was like a diary, only more topical and analytic. John F. Kennedy used his commonplace book to write down phrases that later cropped up in his famous speeches. The practice is not only helpful, it's also healthful. The *Harvard Health Letter* reports that carrying a notebook and jotting down observations is a practice that reduces stress. Keeping a scrap book is a kindred home-based hobby that, in addition to comments noted, also makes room for photos and other souvenirs.

In our digital age, it's possible to use the point-and-click dimension of our computers for notational collecting of verbal text and visual image. Collections are all over the web. Sites such as Collection a Day 2010 *www.collectionaday.com* or Things Organized Neatly *http://thingsorganizedneatly.tumblr.com* show beautiful photographs of collections that you can enjoy without owning any of the stuff. These digital representations of stuff give us the pleasure of collecting without the expense or bother of the physical stuff. It's also possible to turn the smart phone into a digital commonplace book for comments, observations, pictures, and messages sent and received.

Collecting Stories

Lily likes to collect comic strips that she finds particularly funny or insightful. Every day she reviews the newspaper to see what might be fun to cut out. But she doesn't keep very many of these strips. Mostly, Lily passes them along to friends who would value the particular theme or insight, or she includes them in correspondence with family and friends. In our smart-phone era, we can share the comic without bringing out the scissors.

Our friend, Logan, collects stories in the same spirit as Lily saves those comic strips. This hobby makes Logan a good listener, because he loves to assimilate stories told by others. As a callow youth, Logan kept a "humor" file in his desk drawer, but now his lifetime of experiences and listening enables him to keep it all in his head. He's in the position of comedian Rodney Dangerfield who once asked Tonight-Show host Johnny Carson to name a category and he'd supply the jokes. "You want dog jokes, Johnny, I've got dog jokes!" For those who lack the lifetime savvy of Logan and Rodney, it's now possible to use electronic resources such as Evernote *www.evernote.com* to store, search, and access stories.

Collecting for Others

Lily's collecting comic strips for distribution to others illustrates the wider principle that shopping and collecting need not be for ourselves. Remember Grandpa John's hobby of buying miscellaneous boxes at estate sales? John was a strong and vigorous fellow who was not intimidated by heavy boxes of books that sometimes could be had for as little as 25¢. John kept very few of the books. Rather he sorted them by category and appropriately passed them along according to the interests of others. He became so well known as the Johnny Appleseed of books that, at his retirement dinner, his colleagues in the audience— more than 100 of them—stepped forward to present him with a volume to enjoy in his retirement.

Trading Up

There's even a kind of trading that is exactly the same as collecting—trading up. To "trade up" is to improve the quality, but not the quantity, of your collection. How this works is illustrated by our friend, Gavin. We once asked him how he had amassed such exceptionally beautiful collection of objects that would be at home in a museum. Gavin explained that dealers advised him never to sell an antique, but to "trade up." Sometimes Gavin would trade two less-valuable pieces for one of greater quality, and sometimes he would use a trade-plus-extra-cash approach. The result was a lifetime of collecting without increased accumulation. And the approach is practical as well. In every collecting category, the most valuable items are the ones most likely to increase in price over time.

Collections based on an approach opposite to that of Gavin's are more likely to be reported in the media than to qualify for a museum. Consider the case of Charlotte Lee who won fame in the *Guinness Book of World Records* for her rubber duck collection. She owns 5,239 of them and continues to add new ones. "We seem like normal people until you see our basement."[6] Maybe Charlotte is ready to reduce her collection by focusing on quality and not size.

"It's sort of terrible being a collector—I guess because you don't own your things, they own you" according to Peter Potter.[7] To this cautionary note we would add—but not if you trade up!

The Stuff-Cure method of collecting is a kind of un-collecting because the focus is on the activity rather than the result. Why not apply this approach to your entire household of possessions? Focus on experiences rather than things; look for opportunities to substitute notes and pictures for objects; share your things with others; and trade up.

GETTING HELP FROM A PROFESSIONAL ORGANIZER

From everything we've said thus far in the book, the Stuff Cure represents a do-it-yourself project. But we want to alert you to the fact that outside help is available from professional organizers. According to the National Association of Professional Organizers (NAPO), an organizing expert is someone who assists individuals and/or businesses in upgrading their surroundings through categorization, de-cluttering, cleaning, and the application of organizational principles. It's all about enhancing time, productivity, and efficiency.

As with a personal trainer who helps with exercise and fitness, professional organizers serve as a coach. Not only do they provide a storehouse of tips derived from experience, but they are there to encourage when you falter. Looked at according to the three criteria for what to keep, a professional organizer (1) can help you focus on functionality; (2) may have a lot of good ideas about how to maximize income from resale and donation; and (3) won't be overly sentimental about your things.

You can find a list of Professional Organizers near you home at the website of the National Association of Professional Organizers *www.napo.org*. You can also find organizers in your area by looking at classified ads under "Organizing Services." Once you have found some names, interview candidates to find someone who will be a good fit for your personal objectives. Most likely you'll want a person who specializes in residential organizing. You may also want a professional organizer for your office space. A kindred association, The National Study Group on Chronic Disorganization *http://www.nsgcd.org/* makes available a list of its graduates. NSGCD lists a chronic disorganization scale that you can use to assess where you fit on the scale of organization-disorganization, *http://www.nsgcd.org/resources/clutterhoardingscale.php*.

Why take the trouble? A 2009 NAPO membership survey identified the following as the top reasons that Americans hire professional organizers: too much clutter; general disorganization; difficulty determining what to keep and/or discard; difficulty finding things; or selling a home or moving. The top areas in a home where organizing services are most often requested are these: (1) home-office or den; (2) kitchen; (3) closet; (4) master bedroom; and (5) garage/attic/basement.[8]

Anticipating retirement and needing organizational help in connection with a move? The National Association of Senior Move Managers *www.nasmm.org* focuses on helping people downsize as they make moves in their senior years. This organization may help you locate just the right person to help in your situation.

Embarrassed to have a professional look at your clutter and miscellaneous stuff? Remember, professional organizers have seen many peoples' homes and are not likely to be surprised by what they find in your home. After all, it's not like you're inviting in a film crew for some perverse reality show. But it is good to make sure that you and any hired organizer are clear on what you want. Otherwise you may find yourself going along with recommendations that you're not comfortable with as in a *New York Times* article entitled "Abandon All Nostalgia. The Organizer is Coming Over."[9] In this connection, it's more likely that your organizing professional will usefully broker different points of view about stuff held by different members of the household.

PREPARING FOR THE FUTURE

The size of the average American home expanded from 983 square feet, in 1950, to 2,340 square feet, in 2004.[10] The Great Recession of 2008 caused many people to reevaluate the longstanding belief that the bigger the house the better the investment. By 2010, the American Institute of Architects discovered that 57 percent of architecture firms were decreasing the square footage of homes they designed. Industry professionals estimate that, by 2015, the average home will be 2,150 square feet, with living rooms combined with kitchens and family rooms to create a single great room.[11]

What's the right stuff for the next stage in your future?

In the context of the shrinking American home, the Stuff Cure has arrived just in time. The functional orientation of the Cure invites you to embrace the notion that as our needs for stuff change, so too does the stuff. From this point of view, everything owned is held on a temporary basis solely to support us at each phase of our lives. As we change, we need to wring out the old stuff and ring in the new.

Stuff for Your Twenties, Thirties, and Forties

As young adults in our 20s, we want the latest fashion and technology. We're likely to have strong opinions about which stuff appropriately expresses our personality and the image that we want to project. At this stage of life, only our financial resources limit our desire to acquire stuff. We also have the advantage that with our youth, beauty, and enthusiasm, the entire world and all its accoutrement look new and very attractive.

As we age into our 30s, selecting and having stuff helps us signal our status as full-fledged adults. With better jobs and more money, we can choose those items that say to us and to our parents that we have arrived. This is the time when people typically buy their first houses, first sofa set, and expensive refrigerator. Having acquired more big, heavy, expensive stuff, we can no longer move to a new location by piling things in the trunk or back seat of our car.

Like most other young couples of our generation, we began married life with Austin Powers-era stuff that included a fondue set and other such equipment and decorations that looked perfectly in sync with the orange and brown shag carpet. And we certainly couldn't have done without that specialized shag rake that kept the long strands of the carpet in order. Because these were the days before the Stuff Cure, we parted with the rake a residence or two after the last shag, but the fondue set stayed around much longer because the kids got a kick out of it. Finally, a few years after we both had become lactose intolerant, we bit the bullet and donated the fondue pot and forks.

It's not uncommon for folks to enter their 40s with a desire to recapture youth by means of things. Results might include a motorcycle or a trip to Paris. People in their 40s tend to convince themselves that they deserve the best of everything. No wonder that statistics show consumer spending peaking at age 46.[12]

After the 40s peak, people typically continue to consume and acquire because of a common belief that, if they are ever going to have something, the time is now. For us, the result was a sports car, grand piano, and house more than three times bigger than the one we raised our kids in.

Stuff for Your Fifties and After

For many people, a kind of detachment from things begins to set in after age 50, probably because people have finally become comfortable with who they are. A study by the Gallup organization showed that Americans enter adulthood at age 18 feeling pretty good about themselves. But with all the curves that life throws at us, people often report feeling worse and worse about themselves until they hit 50. A sharp reversal occurs at 50, and people report feeling happier as they age. It may surprise you to know that, according to Gallup, people aged 85 are even more satisfied with themselves than they were at 18.[13]

Isn't it interesting that people report more life satisfaction in the decades after their peak purchasing years? Maybe the Stuff Cure is simply part of a natural process of human maturation. After all, at age 60, it's common for people to find their spiritual growth outweighing the need for more physical possessions. Here we increasingly derive our joy from relationships. This may be what drives the urge to be of service to others—as volunteer counselors, docents, or community workers.

The 60s/70s are a time when we're likely to hear people enthusing over the joy of moving from two cars to one, a bigger house to a smaller, and donating instead of buying. Have you heard the old saying that, for boaters, the second happiest day of their life was the day they bought their boat—and the happiest was the day they sold the boat? Every year, this begins to make more sense to us.

Confucius said that life begins at 70, and that only those worthy of life achieve that milestone. Every faith tradition we know of teaches that worthiness relates to spiritual development rather than the acquisition of stuff. Again, Nature seems to help because people in their 80s/90s naturally begin to slow the pace of their life, a metamorphosis that corresponds to needing fewer possessions. This may be a time of a move to assisted living where in-house activity and communal dining bring a lessened need for household goods. This is a time when people may be well along in a process of giving treasured family heirlooms to those with an appreciation for family heritage.

At age 91, the writer Diana Athill describes the Less-Is-More philosophy that comes with wisdom and a smaller place. Athill moved from her apartment into an "old person's home," and described what her smaller surroundings have come to mean. "Everything, from the carpet to the biscuit tin and including, of course, the too many pictures, ornaments and books, is here because however uninteresting it might be to others, I love it." "It's as though 'possessing' has been distilled down from being a vague pleasure to an intense one. Less is more."[14]

Statistics tell us that people are living longer than ever before. What stuff will we need to equip us fully for that future that may include the century mark? No one can give a pat answer to such a question. But this we know. As people age, relationships, spirituality, and wisdom increase in importance. It's likely that as enlightenment becomes the objective, the Stuff Cure will be part of the continuing journey.

• thestuffcure •

EPILOGUE:
FUN, PROFIT, VIRTUE, AND A BETTER WORLD

In the Prologue, we explained our discovery of four outcomes of an Unstuffed Life: fun, profit, virtue, and a better world. This we learned from our own experience of beginning with a house overflowing with four tons of extra clutter—a condition that signalized a life burdened by too much stuff.

FUN

Even when we resolve to downsize and organize, it soon becomes clear that our motivation butts up against heavy realities. In our own case, we admit to finding the process to be daunting in view of our basement and garage brimming with our own and our boys' things, along with stuffed rooms, packed closets, and full shelves. Yet as we enjoyed the success of reducing our inventories a little more each day, we found that renewed energy accompanied our progressively lighter burden. Further, we experienced the inspirational sensation of expediting our voyage to the future by scraping away barnacles of clutter.

And there are some other fun elements to unstuffing. It's a license to play with your long-unused things and to share stories associated with each item. As we placed these extras on the to-be-donated pile, increasingly we felt more in control of our lives. Sometimes we experienced a kind of giddiness when, in one swoop, we could move along a whole category. After getting out the Legos for our visiting boys (who made the decision of what to keep or donate), seven medium-sized movers boxes—gone!

As we've mentioned before, our breakthrough moment in stuff-downsizing occurred in the context of our preparing to move across the country from Missouri to California. Every time we dispensed with something unneeded or unused, we enjoyed anticipating what would be just right for our smaller California home. Sometimes unstuffing was associated with exchanging the obsolete old for the functional new. It was a perfect time for us to discard the old cathode-ray-tube TVs in favor of new flat-screen ones. Just as a meal tastes all the better when we're really hungry, we found we enjoyed shopping more as we were buying only things which would be currently functional.

If you're like us, you may find that embarking on a Stuff-Cure journey brings up the question of what really makes a person happy? "In my experience, the more people have the less likely they are to be contented," says Dr. Andrew Weill in his book *Spontaneous Happiness*. Continuing, Weill makes the point that "Indeed, there is abundant evidence that depression is a 'disease of affluence.'"[1]

The idea of depression amid affluence makes clear that stuff is not the same as life. Take the case of Adi Ellad, who tragically lost his home to the Tujunga Canyon fire of 2009. Among his losses were two items that he particularly cherished—an heirloom Persian rug and a photo album that he put together after his father died. Losing these two items that he assumed he'd own forever caused Adi to reflect, powerfully, on life. "I'm going to have to figure out a new philosophy: how to live without loving stuff," he said.[2]

Experiencing the limitations of things brings up, again, the strong correlation between real happiness and meaningful relationships. People commonly report that money spent for an experience shared with loved ones—such as concert tickets or a vacation trip—produces longer-lasting satisfaction than money expended on plain old stuff.[3] You might find it worthwhile to survey the happiness research conducted by Elizabeth W. Dunn, Daniel T. Gilbert, and Timothy D. Wilson on this topic, *http://dunn.psych.ubc.ca/files/2011/04/Journal-of-consumer-psychology.pdf*.

Moreover, researchers tell us that the meaning of happiness is not fixed; instead, it systematically shifts over the course of one's lifetime. Whereas younger people are more likely to associate happiness with excitement, as people age they place greater stress on peacefulness. This change appears to be driven by a redirection of attention from the future to the present as people age.[4]

For us, happiness includes a daily walk along the Monterey Bay, a beautiful stretch of shoreline near our California home. One day—in fact it was Friday, July 31, 2009—a man wearing an army T-shirt walked up to us and asked if he could take our picture. Question: "Why would you want our picture?" Answer: "You two just look so happy. I hope people would say that my wife and I look as happy as you do." Our passing friend didn't ask us for our philosophy of life. But when we reflected on it, clearly our contented countenances testified to the effectiveness of a life focused on what is important. Fun born of focusing on the essentials is basic to how the Stuff Cure works.

PROFIT

Benjamin Franklin famously wrote that "a penny saved is a penny earned." His maxim certainly applies to those who live an Unstuffed Life. We've already shared with you our calculation that net gains from just our 2008 pre-move downsizing amounted to at least $10,000. Not only have we continued the process since then, but we would calculate our total profit not only in terms of dollars but also from gains that include insights and satisfaction. Gains from sale and donation—10 Grand. Gains from knowledge of what makes us happy—Priceless.

Here it's useful to add a cautionary note that selling sometimes can disappoint if we measure our receipts only against what we originally paid for it new. Fortunately, by the time we were downsizing in 2008, we had long learned to assess old property more realistically—and to measure our gains accordingly. One important learning about realistic value came from an episode some years previously.

We once had occasion to correspond with a china replacement service (this was in the pre-Internet era) about selling a set of our dishware. Knowing that professional packing would decrease our profits, Mike spent an entire morning carefully packing the dishes for shipment, and he wrote a $40 check to cover the cost of shipping the heavy box. The result? Soon our payment for the dishes arrived with an itemized explanation of why we had received a grand total of $43. Seems that some of the dishes were not quite up to par, even though we had sorted out pieces with obvious chips. Our net cash gain of $3.00 meant that, if we credit Mike's packing as worth a dollar per hour, we had essentially donated the dishes by just recovering our shipping costs. We had to laugh, but on balance, we still considered the episode a win. After all, not only had we removed from the house unneeded and heavy dishware, we had learned something about selling old property. By 2008, we had gotten rather better at maximizing returns from sales and donations.

VIRTUE

Our $3.00 profit from selling an entire set of dishes represented for us a life lesson in acceptance. Seen from the highest perspective, letting go of things means recognizing that we've overvalued what we own. All this is part of the detachment from the material world commonly associated with the idea of virtue. It's hard to succeed in virtue and right living if you don't recognize what is important. Finding what is vital and good in life is a subject frequently explored in literature. Take the several novels of Jane Austen that, in addition to being read for nearly two centuries, have been brought to the screen in recent years. In *Sense and Sensibility,* the villainous Fanny Dashwood and Lucy Steele are greedy, materialistic—ever seeking to acquire what isn't rightly theirs. The virtuous Elinor Dashwood and Edward Ferrars maintain integrity, limit their excesses, and focus on human relationships over worldly products.

> **SHARING THE *STUFF CURE***
>
> *Now that you have read the Stuff Cure, consider passing along this book to someone else. Here's your chance to be a bigger part of the solution.*

Faith traditions from across the world seem to agree that detachment from material embellishment is part of a path toward the divine. The sparse living quarters of Junipero Serra, founder of the California missions—now on display at the Carmel, California mission—contains only a wooden bed with a single blanket and a crucifix hung on the wall. Father Serra's environment reflected his recognition that, as Buddha described it, the principal cause of human suffering is attachment to things worldly. Or in the words of Paul, "the love of money is the root of all evil."[5]

Buddha advised cultivating "non-attachment" in order to develop the enlightened mind. Here the Stuff Cure encourages you to identify, and let go of, what is the unnecessary stuff in your life—hanging onto only what sustains you and gives meaning. As you assess your obvious clutter and more subtle storehouses, some of these physical trappings may begin to appear to you as excessive affluence or conspicuous consumption. We do not claim that Stuff-Cure practitioners will immediately attain virtue at the level of Junipero Serra, Buddha, St. Paul, or even the thoughtful and selfless Elinor Dashwood. Yet we do feel that aspiring to live an Unstuffed Life puts us on a better path towards increased virtue. Every time we push material things to the periphery of life, we become better able to emphasize the spiritual.

A BETTER WORLD

Clearly the Stuff Cure represents an individual and personal journey for every person or family. But it's also useful to think about what the world might look like if more people tried to live an Unstuffed Life. Something called the Story of Stuff Project directly addresses this question. The 20-minute video, available at Story of Stuff *http://www.storyofstuff.com/,* encompasses fives stages: extraction; production; distribution; consumption; and disposal. It soon becomes clear in this scenario that the current rate of our consumption does not point to a sustainable future. So maybe it's a good thing that the Stuff-Cure-friendly message of this website has been viewed over seven million times.

If you think about it, everything in life seems to be based on a kind of balance. Life partners need to balance their own individual growth with the growth of their beloved. Parents must integrate their duty to give guidance with the child's need for increasing freedom. And, although politics often emphasizes self-centeredness, Americans commonly recognize that a dictatorship of one group brings disaster. Similarly, while a buyer-driven economy holds sway from New York to Beijing, it's often the case that consumers are attracted by the vision of a leaner, simpler life.

We frankly believe that the world will be a better place if the principles of the Stuff Cure begin to play a larger role in the process of consumption. On a personal level, our cluttered rooms and packed cabinets become opportunities for thrift on our part and, for others, meaningful gifts and donations. From the perspective of the planet, we move in the direction of a more sustainable model of human existence. Reflecting the interconnectedness of life, our world-impacting stewardship of stuff includes moderated consumption (refraining, restraining, returning), efficient consumption (reusing, renting), and end-use consumption (recycling).

As we become better stewards of stuff, everybody benefits. We ourselves focus more on what is important—basic living, relationships with others, generosity to others, and the welfare of the planet with our children and grandchildren in mind. At the same time, transferring the value of stuff to charitable causes supports a wealth of important life-affirming undertakings.

CONTINUE THE CONVERSATION
Want to become part of the Right-Stuff community?

Post your thoughts at *www.StuffCure.com*
to share your experiences and inspiration.

For more information and to book
Betty A. and J. Michael Sproule
for a speaking engagement, visit
www.StuffCure.com
or email *StuffCure@gmail.com.*

We invite you to form, and to focus on, a vision of what the world would be like if more people led an Unstuffed Life. As we cast our own gaze ahead, we picture a cleaner, more beautiful Earth, with more people sharing in a sustainable abundance. We see an emphasis on people and relationships, with stuff serving more as means than end. We hope that the Stuff Cure will help you toward greater personal and interpersonal fulfillment.

• thestuffcure •

END NOTES

Chapter 1 Loving and Hating Our Stuff

1. "Parking Issues," Monterey County Herald, May 13, 2011, Real Estate Section, p. 4.
2. "The Self Storage Self," New York Times Magazine, September 8, 2009, p. 26.
3. "The Self Storage Self," New York Times Magazine, September 8, 2009, p. 27.
4. *http://www.georgecarlin.com.*
5. New York Times, September 30, 2010, p. D11.
6. "The Self Storage Self," New York Times Magazine, September 8, 2009, p. 27.
7. New York Times San Francisco Arts Monthly, October, 2010, vol. 20, no.1, p.12.
8. Much Ado About Nothing, Act iii. Sc. 3.
9. Michele Lerner, The Washington Times, November 28, 2008, p. E1.
10. "The Self Storage Self," New York Times Magazine, September 8, 2009, p. 27.
11. BBC Mobile News Magazine, August 31, 2011, *http://www.bbc.co.uk/news/magazine-14718478.*
12. Nora Ephron, Rob Reiner, Andrew Scheinman, "When Harry Met Sally," 1988, *http://www.imsdb.com/scripts/When-Harry-Met-Sally.pdf.*

Chapter 2 Why Stuff Clings

1. "Smoky Blaze," Monterey County Herald, October 28, 2008, p. A2.
2. "Hoarder May Need Help from Family," Monterey County Herald, March 1, 2010, p.A3.
3. "The Self Storage Self," New York Times Magazine, September 8, 2009, p. 29.
4. "Storage Auctions Abound," San Jose Mercury News, May 10, 2009, p.3E.
5. *http://www.georgecarlin.com.*
6. "Dealing with your Mates' Hideous Pre-couple Stuff," Monterey County Herald, March 6, 2010, p. C3.
7. "Organize This," New York Times, January 9, 2011, p. 23, *http://www.nytimes.com/2011/01/09/nyregion/09organizer.html.*

Chapter 3 Knowing What to Keep

1. "Give Your Wardrobe a Brand-New Start." USA Weekend, August 19-21, 2011, p. 7, *http://www.amazon.com/Have-Nothing-Wear-Painless-clutter/ dp/1605290777/ref=sr_1_1?s=books&ie=UTF8&qid=1314838328&sr=1-1*.
2. "Betting on Beanie Babies," Antique Week, February 15, 2010, p. 23.
3. "From Stratosphere to Donation Bin," Antique Week, November 15, 2010, p. 3.
4. "Will an Online Die Cast Auto Dealership Work?" Antique Week, November 1, 2010, p. 4.
5. "That $5 Shirt? It was Frank Sinatra's," Monterey Herald, July 23, 2010, p. B3.

Chapter 4 Finding a Better Home for Stuff: Gift, Shift, and Thrift

1. "Dear Abby," Monterey County Herald, March 14, 2012, p. 3.
2. "Bartering Makes a Comeback," Monterey County Herald, December 24, 2010, p. C5.
3. Bloomberg Businessweek, July 25-31, 2011, p. 22.
4. "Dear Abby," Monterey County Herald, May 23, 2011, p. B13.
5. "The Booming Flea Markets of New York City," New York Times, May 15, 2011, p. 27.
6. "Bartering Makes a Comeback," Monterey County Herald, December 24, 2010, p. C5.
7. "Pawned," New York Times Magazine, May 15, 2011, p. 20.
8. "Selling J.R., Lock, Stock and Swagger," New York Times, June 4, 2011, p. C1.
9. "A Windfall in Hard Times," New York Times, December 23, 2010, p. D7.

Chapter 5 Stewardship of Stuff: The Seven Morphs

1. USPS 10-K Annual Report 2010, November 15, 2010, *http://www.postalreporternews.net/2010/11/15/usps-annual-report-2010- highlights/*.
2. "Stop! You Can't Afford It," Newsweek, November 7 & 14, 2011, p. 54.
3. See: *http://unconsumption.pbworks.com/w/page/13964615/FrontPage*.
4. "As Economy Worsens, Neighbors Buy, Share Gear," Monterey County Herald, May 22, 2009, p. B1.
5. "House-to-House Hamsters," Monterey County Herald, May 26, 2009, p. B5.

6. "'Reusable Usables' Giving New Life to Old Throwaways," Antique Week, November 8, 2010, p. 16.

7. "Metropolitan Diary," Ricki Fier letter, New York Times, June 8, 2009, p. A14.

8. "Luxuries for Rent Getting Trendy," Monterey County Herald, June 30, 2009, p. B1.

9. "Transforming Trash," Monterey County Herald, September 27, 2011, p. B1.

10. "Tackling High-Tech Trash," San Jose Mercury News, January 10, 2010, p. C1.

11. "A Reason Not to Take Out the Trash," USA Today, July 22, 2010, p. 3A.

12. EPA Report: Quantity of Municipal Solid Waste Generated and Managed, 05/20/2008, *http://cfpub.epa.gov/eroe/index.cfm?fuseaction=detail. viewInd&showQues=Land&ch=46,47,48,49,50&lShowInd=200, 201,202, 203,205,208,209,210,211,225,28,246,281,287,313,315,341,342,343, 381,405&subtop=312&lv=listlistByQues&r=163726.*

Chapter 6. Planning for Progress: The Stuff Cure Method

1. Psalms 37:1, King James Version.

2. "When the Time for Stuff is Over," New York Times, November 25, 2010, p. D1.

3. "Six Easy Pieces, 31 Challenging Days," New York Times, July 22, 2010, p. E6.

4. Barbara Quinn, Monterey County Herald, January 5, 2011, p. C3.

5. "The Show Stopper," Allure, July 11, 2011, p. 112, *http://arabia.msn.com/ Entertainment/Music/covermg/2011/April/4468841.aspx?ref=hptab.*

Chapter 7 Living the Cure — Room by Room

1. Architectural Digest, February 2011, p.110.

2. *http://findarticles.com/p/articles/mi_m1571/is_18_17/ai_74440082/.*

3. "Beloved Books: A Special Spring Cleaning Challenge," Monterey County Herald, March 26, 2011, p. C1.

4. *http://www.careerbuilder.com/share/aboutus/pressreleasesdetail. aspx?id=pr647&sd=7/21/2011&ed=12/31/2011&siteid=cbpr&sc_cmp1=cb_ pr647.*

5. "Bedtime Stories," New York Times, July 25, 2010, p. SS2.

6. "Six Easy Pieces, 31 Challenging Days," New York Times, July 22, 2010, p. E6.

7. http://findarticles.com/p/articles/mi_m1571/is_18_17/ai_74440082/.
8. "Elizabeth Taylor, Close Up," Architectural Digest, July 2011, p. 69.
9. http://en.wikipedia.org/wiki/Cosmetics.
10. Kathy Peel, "Curbing Kids' Clutter," American Profile, March 20-26, 2011, p.14, http://www.americanprofile.com/articles/5-rules-for-kids-rooms.
11. "Parking Issues," Monterey County Herald Real Estate, May 13, 2011, p. 4.

Chapter 8 Doing It Unstuffed

1. "Holiday Shopping on a Budget," USA Weekend, November, 19-21, 2010, p. 8.
2. Terri Orbuch, New York Times, February 12, 2011, p. B5.
3. "When Love Outgrows Gift-Giving," New York Times, February 12, 2011, p. B5.
4. Viviana A. Zelizer, "The Best Present Money Can Buy," New York Times, January 7, 2011, p. A19.
5. Marie Kimball, Thomas Jefferson's Cook Book (Charlottesville, VA: University of Virginia Press, 1976), p. 3.
6. "Edit Well When Putting Collections on Display," Monterey County Herald, October 22, 2011, p. C1.
7. "The Art of Living Well," New York Times, September 8, 2011, p. D5.
8. NAPO 2009 Member Survey 06/30/2009, www.napo.net.
9. "Trust the Professional, It's Time to Toss It Out," New York Times, January 9, 2011, p. 23, http://www.nytimes.com/2011/01/09/nyregion/09playroom.html?ref=nyregion.
10. "Living Well in Less Space," Monterey County Herald, March 5, 2011, p. C1.
11. "Home Builders Look to a Smaller Future," Monterey County Herald, October 29, 2011, p. C1.
12. "Boomer Bears," Newsweek, June 29, 2009, p. 18.
13. "Happiness May Come with Age, Study Says," New York Times, June 1, 2010, p. D5.
14. "In Life's Latest Chapter, Feeling Free Again," New York Times, October 11, 2010, p. C1.

Epilogue Fun, Profit, Virtue, and a Better World

1. "Don't Let Chaos Get You Down," Newsweek, November 7 & 14, 2011, p. 9.
2. "Wildfire's Wrath," San Jose Mercury News, September 1, 2009, p. A6.

• thestuffcure •

3. "But Will It Make You Happy?" New York Times, August 8, 2010, p. BU1.
4. Research findings of Cassie Mogilner, Sepandar D. Kamvar, and Jennifer Aaker, *http://www.dailygood.org/more.php?n=4777*.
5. First Epistle of Paul to Timothy 6:9, King James Version.

• thestuffcure •

INDEX

• thestuffcure •

• thestuffcure •

• thestuffcure •

19850386R00110

Made in the USA
Charleston, SC
14 June 2013